GET MEN
TO WANT YOU

Michael Anthony

The Institute of Human Understanding

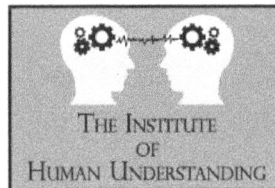

The Institute
of
Human Understanding

INTRODUCTION

Getting a man to want you isn't hard if you're willing to accept less than you want or deserve. Settling for less than you want or deserve is unacceptable. Getting the right man isn't easy. Numerous factors play into getting the right man to want you. These factors include timing, presentation, and a connection. Ultimately, to get the right man, you must garner the right type of attention from him, and you must deserve it. This book outlines how to not only deserve it but also demand it without saying a word.

In our fast-paced lives, everyone wants everything now. Unfortunately, people are impatient. Men are no exception, they think by simply telling a woman she's hot or going on one date, they deserve to get something in return. These men need training to think differently and act differently. You'll learn how to train them, without their feeling you're doing it. This is covert persuasion, and it's amazing.

To get a better idea on Michael Anthony's story and why he's the right person to lead you, you need to learn more about him. He was young when his parents divorced, and his single attractive mother raised him. He routinely witnessed men approach her and how she responded to their "game." Their house was the gathering spot for all her friends, which would inevitably lead to "girl talk." Frankly, he heard way too much. It was clear from an early age, men will do and say almost anything to a woman, sincere or not.

With this knowledge in mind, he absorbed interactions both personally and from afar with a keen interest, while reading extensively on psychology. As his friends started to develop an interest in girls, he became the go-to person to help them. He also became great friends with many girls who were experiencing problems and settling for far less than they deserved. This was a hot button for Michael since he didn't believe in settling and made it a point to help them do better to be happier.

Michael was clearly ahead of his time with his adaptation and vision of using online sites and apps. As a teenager, he began advising friends on using Myspace to meet women back in the early 2000s. He saw the potential with meeting online. Sure, styles have changed, technology has advanced, and our lives have gotten even busier, but having kept a pulse on all this along the way has allowed Michael to become more efficient in his approach.

With dating sites and apps taking over the dating scene, now more than ever women need direction in how to get the right guy. While happily married himself, Michael is still actively helping friends. Having experienced the hanging out, dating, married, and family stages has given Michael a unique perspective to help women experience the lives they want and soon will deserve.

New apps and online dating sites are being created daily. Many will come, and most will go. The strategies, insights and analysis provided within this book are universal. They have stood the test of time and are currently working today.

This book is only for those wanting to improve their lives and get men to want them. If this is you, welcome and we're happy you're here.

Tera Allison

Contents

SECTION I:

WHY ONLINE DATING
AND DATING APPS

CHAPTER 1:
ONLINE DATING AND DATING APPS MAKE SENSE FOR YOU

"Online dating and dating apps are the only true option if you value your time."

—Michael Anthony

You're busy. Driving in traffic is frustrating, working overtime has become the norm, and finding time to go grocery shopping is a chore. With the constant drains on your time and attention, how can you expect to find a man?

Finding a man could be a full-time job. There are men who will waste your time, will tell you what you want to hear, outright lie, and try to play you. Simply put, there are many types of men to avoid and even more issues to steer clear of in the dating world.

For these reasons, online dating and dating apps have taken over. As with all advances in technology, dating has become easier to do with less of a time commitment. However, you must know how to navigate it to maximize your results and minimize wasted time.

This book does just that. It navigates you through the sites and apps to use and helps you to identify the different types of men, to lead conversations without their knowing you're in control, and, ultimately, to get men to want you.

The reality is most men are not initially looking for a relationship. Though, the right woman can trigger any man to commit to a relationship. Think of Hugh Hefner.

Women are as guilty as men, if not more guilty, in playing games, leading others on, and wasting time.

Despite your parents telling you that you were perfect as you grew up, you're not. You have flaws and that's okay. The coddling received by parents often backfires against the very person they were trying to protect—you.

Men aren't going to view you and tell you regularly that you're beautiful when you aren't wearing makeup, have baggy sweatpants on with an oversized T-shirt, like mommy and daddy will or did. The issue isn't that men won't tell you this, the issue is you're looking for them to tell you that you're beautiful or pretty. You don't need their approval; if you look and feel your best, their compliments are a bonus.

For this reason, we detail within this book how to show your best features, minimize the worst features, and display yourself in the best light. You can only do this through an honest evaluation of yourself. By being honest, you will grow in all areas and be the best you.

Being the best you will help elevate yourself in the dating world. Think of your online dating profile as your resume. You don't want to put too much or come across as just another option. You want to come across as a great option, one that someone doesn't want to miss out on. After all, people act more often based on a fear of missing out rather than an urgency. Think of a pair of shoes or clothing item you bought due to its being a great deal or the last one left and others wanting it.

This is the true opportunity these sites and apps provide. You can make decisions quickly, communicate at once and minimize wasted time going on blind dates only to learn they aren't your type for one reason or another.

Gone are the days of going to a bar in the hopes of meeting a decent guy, searching for a date to a wedding or event, vacationing by yourself, and being alone for the holidays.

The times of waiting for a man to approach you, talk to you, or ask you out are behind you. As detailed in this book, online dating sites, dating apps, and stealth sites provide a great opportunity for you to contact them first, as well. Remember, your time is valuable. Don't wait for anything; go get what you want!

CHAPTER 2:
WHAT TO EXPECT

"Don't lower your expectations to meet your performance. Raise your level of performance to meet your expectations."

—Ralph Marston

Men are traditionally very easy to read. They have difficulty displaying self-control in words and through actions when they feel attracted to a woman. This puts a woman at a distinct advantage.

We see this in a social setting regularly. Men purchase drinks for women, offer to spend money, and do anything possible to get their attention. Online, men do the same. However, since it's online, men are limited to words, intelligence, and their profiles. Men can't hide behind a drink.

This is something to be thankful for. The men who aren't at your intellectual level won't waste your time since you can delete their messages with a click of a button. This is one of the first steps to cut the fat from online dating. We'll cover profile design, pictures, messages, and chats later since each of these play a role in determining the right guy for you. The quicker you get rid of the bad, the easier it is to sort through the good.

To gain a better understanding of what a woman experiences when she's on dating sites and apps, I created three different fake profiles on both Plenty of Fish and Match.com over a two-month period. Each profile had five photos, and the "About Me" section had four sentences. I used each of the three profiles for a period of three days in a certain ZIP code. After the three days were up, I used the same profile but changed the ZIP code to a location in another state. After those three days were up, I used the same profile again and changed the ZIP code to yet another, different state. In total, I created 18 profiles: nine for Plenty of Fish and nine for Match.com, although there were only six originals duplicated two additional times to garner response rate.

I followed the same outline regarding age, number of pictures, types of pictures, and wrote four sentences for each profile. To get the pictures, I searched the internet for random pictures. From there, I viewed profiles until I found photos to complement the profiles. I uploaded these photos to each site/app and then typed four sentences in the "about me" section that described each fictional woman as being new to the area with a couple of generic sentences regarding liking the beach and vacationing. Because Plenty of Fish is free, I wasn't under much of a time crunch, but I was with Match since I used the free trial periods.

In total, there were three profiles, each displayed in a total of three states for three days apiece. Within just three days, others viewed the profile 126 times and sent 78 emails and 92 winks. As you can imagine, there was a lot to sort through from the number of emails, winks, and profile views received in just three days. Some of this information was entertaining, to say the least.

To be honest, the response was borderline overwhelming. The messages were a mix of inappropriate, creepy, and predictable. It was clear after this that there had to be a better way for women to sort through the rift raft.

INSTANT MESSAGES

There's an option on Plenty of Fish and many other dating sites/apps to have your settings show if you're online at that moment. You can enable or disable that feature. The instant messenger service allows any person who sees you online to instant message you. Within just 10 minutes, we had to turn off this feature because the number of messages coming in exceeded 20. The instant messages included compliments about "her" looks, simple small talk, pictures of half-naked bodies, and promises to take her on the best date ever. The following are some condensed excerpts of instant messages sent to "her."

- What are you doing tonight gorgeous?
- HEY!
- I think I fell in love once I saw your pictures!
- When are you free to hang out?
- Have you been to the new piano bar?
- I can show you around since you are new to town

TEXT MESSAGES

As if creating a fake profile weren't enough, I then purchased a prepaid phone for each profile. The voicemail was set up with the generic computer automated voice that reads back the phone number as the voicemail greeting, so no voice was present on the voicemail greeting. During the chat and emails, "she" wrote that texting was the best way to contact "her." Though this was pushing my comfort zone, I knew it was necessary for this book to have detailed and accurate case studies.

I specifically asked for a different area code when I purchased the phone and prepaid card that matched the story of recently moving to the area and her area code. As you can imagine, she had quite the array of text messages sent to her. Some were rude, others sounded very desperate, many were inappropriate, and all were very easy to see through.

The following are examples of text messages sent to "her."

- What are you doing?
- Are you busy as you still haven't messaged me back??
- If you don't like me, just tell me...
- Where do you live?
- Are you dating anyone?
- I would satisfy you more than you ever have been before.
- Can't wait to meet you!
- How long have you been single?
- Are you there?

It's safe to say, men need a lot of help in their approach. It's also safe to say women need more help to sort through the messages and men to have success dating online. While there may not be an algorithm to sort through the bad to get the good narrowed down, there is this book. This book will show you step-by-step how to narrow down the overwhelming number of men on sites and apps and continually sort through the options so you only invest your valuable time with those who are worthy of it.

SECTION II:

LEARNING ABOUT MEN

CHAPTER 3:
TYPES OF MEN

"There are two kinds of men. There are men who are fucking misogynist pigs, and then there are men who really love women, who think they're the most amazing people in the world."

—Adam Levine

To understand men, you must properly identify the different types of men. We've broken down the eight different types of men with a description for you to better identify them. This will prove especially useful when you can identify the type of man upon initial meeting, chat, or viewing their profile.

THE EIGHT DIFFERENT TYPES OF MEN

1. Awkward Guy: This guy is socially awkward. He's clueless as to what to say and when. His habits range from being tough on himself and questioning what's wrong with him to blaming others for his lack of success. Rather than improving on any past successes, he psyches himself out before, during, and after any communication. It's common for him to say inappropriate things and appear nervous. This makes any communication he has even more awkward.

2. Clingy Guy: Characteristics include being too emotionally open with the woman from the start. This guy may have wondered why a woman ended a relationship or stopped dating him, although he's not honest with himself. He gets too emotionally involved, which scares a lot of women, and still he remains clueless about what went wrong. He dissects every conversation and moment they were together. The Clingy Guy scares many women away because he compliments them too often and even says, "I love you" quickly. They also make the mistake of offering commitment too quickly by saying, "I'm not seeing anyone else" and "I feel like we were meant to be."

3. Touchy/Feely Guy: The best two words for this guy are *back off*! He starts hugging, holding hands, kissing, and wrapping his arm around a woman at an early stage. This can lead to discomfort, since you may not know him yet and can lead you to question how many other girls he has done this to.

4. Too Intense Guy: He's difficult to handle; he's so invested that he can come across as confrontational. He's rarely calm as his passion doesn't allow him to step back to take a breath. A balance is necessary, and this guy doesn't have it.

Careers most common with this type of man is a sports coach, sales manager, or extreme sport enthusiast.

5. <u>Life of the Party Guy:</u> This guy sees himself as hilarious. He often takes jokes too far. He can be too loud and make offensive comments, which embarrass him and others around him. This person is not comfortable fitting in with the crowd; he craves the attention.

6. <u>Money Bags Guy:</u> This guy likes to overcompensate for his insecurities by flashing money. He may try to impress a woman by taking her to an expensive restaurant, buying drinks, spending cash in excess, and trying to dress and live up to an image he has created for himself.

7. <u>The Natural Guy:</u> This is the guy who has it down. He's a "natural" in a social setting and is rarely uncomfortable, can easily strike up a conversation, and is genuinely enjoyable to be around. Both men and women enjoy his company. He's very smooth with women, without needing to flash money or by not being genuine because he understands how to communicate and interact in a respectful, yet attractive manner.

8. <u>Nice Guy:</u> This guy would be the "perfect gentlemen." He's the image of what most parents teach their sons to be from a young age. He's polite and compliments women often. These compliments include, "You're pretty," "You're beautiful," "You're amazing," and "I like you so much." He opens the door for the woman, treats her like a princess, and, unfortunately for him, he has the "friend" label or referred to as being like a brother.

Chances are you thought of real-life examples of men you know that meet each of the types above. Some men may display multiple characteristics detailed, both good and bad. Since you now understand them in black and white, you must determine what you want and like, to begin your focus on what you will attract.

RED FLAGS—GUYS TO AVOID

- Sexual talk—any man pushing the conversation to sex or anything sexual in nature clearly has one thing on his mind.
- Relationship—if he's in a relationship or is not clearly single, this is a major red flag. Who is to say this isn't a pattern and he isn't still in the relationship? If you were interested or intrigued by this guy, he could easily do the same to you down the road.
- Married—if he acknowledges or if you determine he's still married, stay clear. Despite his stating he's separated, or the divorce isn't final, you're walking into a mess. Save the drama.
- Emotional—if he's quick to get emotional, attached, or reveal too much personal information, be concerned. You're interested in a partner not a patient to counsel.

In Chapter 16 we will cover pictures men post that are red flags.

CHAPTER 4:
THROUGH A MAN'S EYES

"You guys are stereotyping a lot of people."

"Of course, we are. Words do that; that's what words are for. Words generalize experience, but you only need to be offended if they apply to you directly."

—Frogs into Princes by Richard Bandler and John Grinder

Below is the breakdown of how men view women. This is important to review because you must identify where you fit in this mix. Be honest with yourself. You can only improve and see yourself from a different perspective by being truthful. This is self-actualization. As you become more aware of your negative habits and features, you can work on them, while maintaining the characteristics detailed below as positive ones. Simply put, you have many of these characteristics, good and bad. Through self-actualization and discipline, you can show the good ones you may be holding in, i.e. happiness, humility, outgoing, fun.

HOW MEN CLASSIFY WOMEN

TYPE	HIGH MAINTENANCE	NORMAL	LOW SELF-ESTEEM
HIGHLY ATTRACTIVE	Selfish, conceited, rude, inconsiderate, judgmental, and highly critical. She has more opinions and options so will typically reject most men she encounters.	Likeable, humble, enjoyable to be around, and not judgmental. She is a rarity to find because she isn't demeaning to others because she's attractive.	Insecure, hesitant, shy, uncomfortable, and continually seeking approval. She is easily embarrassed with a compliment and most likely has had a bad experience in her childhood or past relationships directly impacting her self-esteem.

TYPE	HIGH MAINTENANCE	NORMAL	LOW SELF-ESTEEM
AVERAGE	Not a "natural" beauty, must work at it, on the surface may appear tough and confident, though still insecure as she remembers how life used to be for her and is still a bit vulnerable behind a "bitchy" persona.	One of the "best" core girls you could find, easygoing in most aspects of life, content in relationships, trustworthy, has substance and good character.	Rarely achieves happiness because she doesn't strive for it. Prefers security and often settles to feel secure. Ends up regretting she never lived to be happy, scared of change, and prefers to play it "safe" and be okay rather than being happy.
BELOW AVERAGE	Perhaps the worst to be around, resembles a dictator, likes to be in charge, will sacrifice a good guy for one who bows to her every command, and thinks she's much better than she is. Men are responsible for creating this monster by the attention they give her.	Because looks are not on her side, she gives attention elsewhere. She's typically an intellectual, a deep thinker, and a dreamer. Tends to be more loyal because she doesn't have as many options and doesn't want to ruin a good thing.	Very indecisive and insecure. Attracted to more decisive men who will make decisions, and she's typically obedient and quiet, - often leading to unhealthy relationships because of her weak nature and being walked all over.

Now that you can see how men classify women, you must now learn how to recognize the characteristics of men to better identify and communicate with each type.

CLASSIFYING MEN—ANALYSIS

HOT

- <u>High maintenance:</u> He knows he's attractive and has plenty of options with women. He may have striking features, is in good physical shape, have good style, and talks with ease.
  <u>Analysis:</u> This is the making of a "playboy" and an asshole. He'll rarely care for your feelings; he's too wrapped up in himself to consider them. While he may be easy on the eyes, he's tough on the mind and heart.

- <u>Normal:</u> A grounded, good person who happens to be very attractive. Despite his physical advantages in the looks department, he still treats others with respect and doesn't act as better than anyone. Typically comes from a more down-to-earth family, where no one told him he was better than anyone else.

Analysis: This is the unicorn for a woman to find. The biggest challenge with this type of guy is that as time passes he understands he has superior looks and many options with women. This can lead to changes in his behavior. The goal for a woman is to identify and secure this man before he has been exposed to the dating world for an extended period.

- Low Self-Esteem: This guy typically is insecure. Other kids may have treated him poorly when growing up or made fun of him for lack of intelligence in school or athleticism or his parents didn't reassure of their love for him. As a result, he hangs his head, has poor posture, and has low expectations of himself.

  Analysis: This man typically ends up with the woman who finds him early and is willing to show him the love and attention he's been missing. Since he has low expectations, he follows his instinct to settle with the first woman who shows an interest in him and willingness to commit first.

AVERAGE

- High Maintenance: He is average in the looks department, though increases his appearance by working on it. He'll dress nicely, appear well-kept, smell good, and work on his physical features, such as tanning, hairstyle, working out, etc. He becomes self-absorbed as his efforts to improve his appearance garner attention, which increases his ego.

  Analysis: This man typically ends up with a woman like himself who also works on her appearance since she values similar things. Think of a bodybuilder's wife; she's typically very in sync with his appearance as well. She's fit, well-kept, eats healthy, wears clothing to flaunt her body, and may have had surgery done to enhance her appearance.

- Normal: He's down-to-earth, not asking much of others, while often shying away from the attention. His ambition doesn't always match his talent, although he finds contentment in everyday life.

  Analysis: This man typically ends up with a woman who's like himself: easygoing, likes the daily status-quo life, and is down-to-earth.

- Low Self-Esteem: This man achieves very little due to the constant drain of his emotions on his personal and professional life. He rarely strives for anything above average since his confidence, or lack of, doesn't warrant it. As a result, he settles for an okay job, okay woman, and okay life.

  Analysis: This man can do much better in all aspects of life –job, significant other, and life. However, due to his limited vision and unwillingness to step out of his borderline depressed outlook, he's stuck living an average life.

BELOW AVERAGE

- High Maintenance: This is a man to avoid. He thinks he's better than he is, has more to offer than he does, and is god's gift to women. Despite his overwhelming confidence, he's still insecure inside. He will spend a lot of money to look his best, but this is an act of insecurity. He's hiding behind the designer clothing and nice car and understands this. For this reason, he continually is looking in the mirror when out in public, readjusting his shirt and appearing a bit uncomfortable in the fashionable clothing he's wearing.

  Analysis: This man may attract someone out of his league, though also high-maintenance or more likely to attract someone like him. They'll also be meticulously groomed—haircuts, shaving, waxing, dressed in designer clothing and always looking their best. However, they both understand they're not natural beauties but will never dare reveal this insecurity to the other person because they'd never want to chance the other person seeing the "real" person.

- Normal: This is a man who flies under most women's radar. He's typically loyal. Despite not being the "hottest" guy in the bunch, he's pragmatic and is a great person to be in a relationship with. He's a decent person who connects with a woman on a deeper level than looks alone, which can lead to a stronger foundation as the attraction can increase over time rather than decrease since looks rarely improve with age.

  Analysis: This man will end up with a woman who appreciates what he has to offer in terms of substance, which will lead to a better relationship moving forward based on their connection.

- Low Self-Esteem: This man is a loner. He rarely speaks to women. When the rare occasion does come about in public, he will typically avoid eye contact and look like a battered puppy. He has little to no confidence, with no understanding how to improve it. He continually worsens his feelings inside by thinking of how other guys have no issues talking to, meeting, and hanging out with women.

  Analysis: His ideal match is a woman with a dominating personality. She will approach him to set up a date, hang out or make any moves such as kissing. This is great for him as she becomes the leader he can follow.

Through my studies, I have found that most women feel more attracted to men who are with other women or other women are pursuing. The reasoning for this is a combination of scarcity and challenge. The concept of scarcity creates a much more desired state since there's very limited supply. The challenging part is just that, a challenge. A woman likes the concept of pursuing a man who may not be interested in her. In fact, women will work harder for a man's attention, simply to prevent another woman from getting it.

You cannot allow this to distract you, and you must discipline your approach based on whether you're interested. Remain disciplined, and you'll be more desirable to the man, since you're not as easy to get as the woman throwing herself at him. Your goal is to be the most desirable. How a man looks at you is how he ultimately will feel about you.

DETAILS, DETAILS, DETAILS

Men may be easy to read in many regards, such as staring at cleavage or a revealing outfit, though they're not as oblivious to the details as women may think.

Men will take notice of the following things:

- <u>Friends</u>—Your friends reflect you. Good quality friends this will pique a man's interest in you. This may be surprising, but if you look at friends you have that are in committed relationships, most of their significant others got along with your group of friends quickly to start.
- <u>Job</u>—is there a future there or is it a job going nowhere. Overall, men feel attracted to what they are. If you're happy with a job with no future, this is the type of man you'll attract. Men who feel motivated by having a better future through a better job and opportunity will attract a woman who's looking for the same.
- <u>Goals</u>—If you don't have goals and are not pursuing them actively, this will be obvious. Lip service is common, actions are not. Actions speak louder than words.
- <u>Drinking</u>—Getting drunk or needing to be the center of attention when drinking will have you come across as a party girl. Sure, men like to hang out with and have fun with party girls, though nothing more than that.
- <u>Appearance</u>—If you take pride in your appearance, it will show. It will also show if you don't. When you look like you just rolled out of bed in wrinkled clothes, hair a mess, and no makeup, a man will see this as a lack of effort on the woman's part. As result, he may either reject this and you as not a good fit for him or accept it and return this lack of effort to you. This is not the road either of you want to go down.

WHAT GUYS FEEL ATTRACTED TO AND WANT

<u>Physical Wow Factor</u>—remember how a guy looks at you is how he thinks about you. If he thinks you're hot, he will associate any thoughts of you with your hot/attractive appearance, which is good.

<u>Character Factor</u>—if you are a solid person in terms of character, a man is likely to initially deflect if he's looking for fun and not substance. However, most of the time men have difficulty passing up a quality woman, so he eventually succumbs to the future consideration. Men appreciate a good woman, and the good women are the ones they tend to end up with. Being a good reflection of a man is good for business, too.

<u>Connection Factor</u>—connecting with a woman is important for a man on a physical and emotional level. Despite the belief that men aren't as emotionally involved or committed as a woman, this is false. Men feel drawn to women, as women feel drawn

to men through an attraction or connection. Common likes, dislikes, and interests create a foundation for future conversations and discussions that lead to cherished experiences.

The Mom Factor—Men are not looking for their moms. They are, however, looking for a woman who has the characteristics they view as good for kids down the road as both a wife and mom. Being nurturing, welcoming, loving, and strong are all characteristics men feel attracted to.

Future Factor—to determine the right move, right fit, and right person in life it comes down to timing. You could find the perfect match but if the timing isn't right, it won't work. For this reason, men feel attracted to women based on their plans, not current life. Their current lifestyle (could be a bachelor life) is not a long-term goal for most men. Finding a woman who will fit into his future goals, whether it be having kids, traveling, business, or getting along with his family and friends are.

SECTION III:

CREATING AND SHOWCASING THE NEW YOU

CHAPTER 5:
BE THE BEST YOU—PHYSICAL TIPS

"Since we cannot change reality, let us change the eyes which see reality."

—Nikos Kazantzakis

To be the best you, you must give your best effort. There are no shortcuts to being successful in life. Luckily for you, being the best you can be and looking your best won't take years. It can take minutes, hours, or days, depending on what you want to be your best. The goal of this chapter isn't to get men to want you; it's to get you to be the best you. As a result, you'll feel better, your confidence will increase, and your life will be better and more enjoyable. The icing on the cake is it will also attract men and get men to want you.

GROOMING

The goal is to work with your flaws not against them and to minimize them.

1. Shaving—shave regularly all part(s) of the body below your head you don't wax (legs, armpits, private parts, arms if overwhelmingly hairy). Despite the temptation to let a day or two go, don't give in. You feel better when you look better. When you do shave, have a mental checklist of each area and go over each area multiple times. Furthermore, be sure to check a third time once you're out of the shower.
2. Plucking is painful, though necessary. A unibrow is not attractive, nor are potential hairs on the face. Pluck to remove it and check each morning to maintain. This includes eyebrows and any random hairs on your face—cheeks, forehead, chin, upper lip, etc. Be sure to check your entire body for random dark hairs, some of which can grow out of moles, as well.
3. Breath—bad breath can kill any deal. We all have been around someone with bad breath due to not brushing the night before or after eating a bag of chips—yuck! Always carry floss, a toothpick, and mints/gum with you. Make it a habit to check your teeth after any meal and snack to confirm you don't have anything in your teeth, follow this with a piece of gum or mints.

4. Nails—keep nails neatly trimmed or kept up, if longer. Paint or polish them if they're discolored or bruised. Don't bite your nails; it looks unkempt and unattractive.

5. Teeth—straight teeth are a must. If crooked, see an orthodontist and straighten them; they're one of the first impressions anyone will have with you—in business and in life. Do what it takes to get them straight; your confidence will improve once you notice the impact it has on your appearance. Whiter teeth are also preferable. Whiter teeth stand out, as do yellow or stained teeth. There are many whitening toothpastes and whitening strips on the market today.

6. Hair—always keep hair tidy. The style isn't as important as a well-kept appearance. Messy, frizzy unkempt hair is a turn-off.

7. Hairstyle tips based on face type:
   a. Big ears—wear hair down
   b. Round face—hair up
   c. Big nose—hair up
   d. Bad acne on forehead—never have bangs; they'll cause more problems

8. Make-Up—don't overdo it. Less can be more. Some concealer to cover up a breakout does more harm than good when you cake it on since it brings more attention to it than if you did nothing. Mascara—yes, lipstick—yes, light concealer—yes, though use neutral colors. Avoid the colors that stand out for eye shadow and mascara.

9. Skin—moisturize; smooth skin is attractive. As noted above, you're more likely to notice a flaw than something positive. The same is true for skin. dry, flaky skin will garner negative attention immediately, regardless of the attraction.

10. Skin color—get some sun outside. Having a little bit of color will make you look healthier, feel better, and can make you look thinner as a result. Not everyone wants to go tanning, but a simple walk outside to get sun can do your body some good. Vitamin D is good in the winter months due to the deficiency most people have from lack of sun exposure.

LIFESTYLE

1. Drinking—being a social drinker is different from a partier or an alcoholic. Maintaining self-control eliminates the embarrassment of saying inappropriate things or acting in a manner that leads others to think of you negatively. A man looks at a woman he's willing to commit to different from one he's looking to have fun with. Men don't date, commit, or get married to the party girl.

2. Eating—eating right and taking care of your body is an investment into your future. Outside of the obvious impact on your appearance and health, your energy level will also benefit.

3. Gym—Go! Your goal may not be to be a fitness model, though it can to improve your overall health. The toughest part about going to the gym is going. Once you're there, it becomes a decompressor for many from the everyday stresses of work and life. As you enjoy it, you'll see results. Taking pleasure in going to the gym will also help you stay committed. When a man sees you going to the gym regularly, they'll notice you're taking care of yourself. This can result in his seeing the value you place on it, and he may act on his end to better himself. Work on areas that need improvement, don't attempt to hide them with Spanx or something similar because this is like lying. It will eventually be exposed, and

wasting time with false advertisements will impact you negatively in the long term. Just as you wouldn't want a guy to wear a compression belt to hide a beer belly, don't give into temptation.

    a. Remember, during the courting stage, you lay the foundation for the dating and relationship stages. These behaviors, traits, and habits will follow any potential future you two may have, which is a good thing. Drinking responsibility, eating right and being healthy is a win/win for all. Have high expectations; both parties will be better off as a result.

CHAPTER 6:

STYLE—GET IT, HAVE IT, SHOW IT

"I have never seen people so satisfied with mediocrity."

—Jack Burns from the movie, Meet the Parents

Style: Not everyone has it, though everyone can learn it. Some may be naturals with putting together an outfit or knowing what looks good, but there are sites, magazines, and blogs that provide you a cheat sheet for what's currently in style. If you prefer to see what the outfits look like on you firsthand, you can simply go to a popular store that has the newest fashions and styles already laid out for you. You're looking for timeless style insights to look your best based on your physical features, eye color, skin tone, body type, and more. It also outlines what men find attractive, so you can cater to your audience.

STYLE POINT #1—COLORS CHOICES

There are so many options with colors today. With multiple shades and versions of each color, you must be more in tune with what looks good and what works for you.

What's in style can also change based on your location. For instance, black, sophisticated style is synonymous with New York City. In contrast, cool, laid back and casual is associated with the California lifestyle. You need to use color to enhance your positive features, not for your location. Sure, classic colors work for certain events, weddings, and funerals, but this is the dating world!

Timeless colors such as black, white, and gray are neutral since they match almost anything. Sure, a floral dress may be in style, though a black dress will be timeless for nearly any occasion. The days of blue eye shadow and perms were popular in the '80s, but those days are gone. The outline below is to help you navigate the colors that work best.

Rule of thumb for picking colors:
- Clothing
  - Eye color—Having a shirt or outfit main color that matches your eye color is the most powerful statement with color; it will enhance your eye color and give you an exotic look.
    - Exotic = different. Different = standing out. Standing out = good.

- o   If you have a darker complexion or are tan, choose lighter colors.
  - ▪ These include pastels, whites, and lighter versions of traditionally dark colors—light gray, etc.
- o   If you have fair skin or a pale complexion, avoid the lighter colors because they'll make the contrast even greater and can wash you out.
  - ▪ Instead, use darker colors such as black, dark gray, navy blue, etc.

- • Hair color—dye
  - o   Coloring one's hair is common. Some like to add color during the summer months, while others like to consistently change their hair color as a hobby.
    - ▪ If you're coloring your full head of hair, make sure you spread the color evenly and cover everything from the tips to the roots. If you don't, it can be darker or appear missed in certain areas.
    - ▪ If you're simply adding streaks or doing highlights, avoid using any drastic colors that clash with your hair. To know whether it will clash with your current hair color, avoid having a streak that isn't in the same tone—dark/dark = okay, light/dark = not okay. If you have light blond hair and you add random streaks of black, it won't look right. But, if you add a nice red/maroon type of streak to darker hair, the change wouldn't be as drastic.

- • Make-up
  - o   Lipstick
    - ▪ Red is the traditional color, but the most attractive color lipstick to men varies. Don't overlook pinks and darker colors as ways to stand out. Just pay attention to the details—no lipstick on teeth, not layered on too thick and be meticulous about having it only on the lips alone, not on any skin surrounding the lips.
  - o   Eyeshadow
    - ▪ Traditional colors are best. Crazy colors will generate stares, not interest. Use colors to make your eyes stand out. For example, if you have blue eyes use gold or green, hazel eyes use purple, and brown eyes use brown. You don't want someone to look at you strictly because you stand out with bright orange eyeshadow.

STYLE POINT #2—UNIVERSAL OUTFIT TIPS

Despite what may be in fashion, very few guys appreciate and feel attracted to baggy, oversized clothing, which comes in and out of popularity regularly. Men do, however, feel attracted to certain types of clothing, colors, and types of outfits. By following the universal tips below, you'll gain valuable insight into getting men to want you.

Universal Outfit tips—for all body types:
- White pants, dresses, and skirts—yes
  - Men always feel drawn to a woman in white pants, dresses, and skirts. Combine this with a nice tan, and you're certain to get men to want you.
- Shirts—baggy shirts are a no.
  - It may be in style to wear a shirt that resembles a poncho, but that doesn't mean a man will find it attractive or appreciate the style sense. Oversized T-shirts and other clothing are also not clothing types recommended.
    - **Note:** Do not wear a dark-colored bra under a light color shirt. This will give the appearance of being trashy and not gain the right kind of attention.
- Skirts—yes
  - A skirt doesn't have to be a short one. One knee length that fits right will be equally, if not more, attractive to most men.
    - **Note:** Do not wear dark-colored underwear if you're wearing a light color skirt.
- Materials matter
  - Not all materials will fit your body type right. The same size and cut will lay over your body and hug other parts differently. This is not a problem with you, it's the reality of mass production of clothing and varying body types. For this reason, take notice of how your clothing look from each angle. Self-awareness is key to not overlooking details that may make you look less desirable. Materials range from cotton, polyester, spandex, cashmere, leather and more—each fitting differently.
    - When you're trying on an outfit, look at yourself directly straight on, from each side, from the back and in different positions. These positions should include sitting on a chair and with your arms straight to your side, folded and with your arm on your hip. This is necessary since they're the most common positions you use, and you need to be more alert than ever moving forward.
- Tank tops—yes and no
  - A tank top may be appropriate for hot weather, so you'll expose your full arms. If you decide to wear a tank top, it's an absolute necessity to have shaved armpits. Not shaved two days ago, freshly shaved that day. It's also okay only if your arms are somewhat toned or in shape.
    - The same rule applies to tank tops and shirts, do not wear a dark-colored bra if you wear a lighter color tank top.
- Classy > Trashy
  - Guideline—Underwear and bras should match shirt or pants/skirts. If not matching, they should never be darker than the shirt or pants. Wearing a dark-colored bra visible through a light color shirt is not a good look. The same is true for underwear readily seen through pants or a skirt. It may get eyes from guys, but not the eyes you want.

- Less is not more. Leave something to the imagination.
  - Showing more skin will not guarantee more attention. It may if you show enough of it, but you must remember what your goal is. If you're looking for a guy interested in a short-term fling, this is a good route to go. If you're looking for better quality men, this is not necessary.
- Future—after you have the guy
  - It's easy to fall into the trap of dressing differently and not attempting to impress a man, once you feel as though he's yours. This is detrimental to the dynamic between the two of you. Remember, both parties will copy the mannerisms and actions of the others. If you look your best, it will yield him doing more to look his best. If you appear to have given up, he'll quickly do the same.
  - If you want to keep your guy and want your guy to stay as interested in you as he was at the start, stay on top of your game. Give the attention to keeping him as you did with looking your best for all the losers you met along the way.

STYLE POINT #3—DRESSING YOUR BODY TYPE

Each woman has features she feels are attractive and others they're insecure about. The outline below is meant to help you look your best, while still being comfortable. Not everyone is comfortable in a skin-tight body dress, and that's understandable. The belief growing up among women is that thin is good. This is the reason society pushes diet and exercise on young girls at an early age. However, times have changed with the expectation of looking like a Barbie doll.

A perfect example of this is Kim Kardashian. She has become the Marilyn Monroe sex symbol of today. Many who dislike her are quick to comment about her not being thin or in good shape. She doesn't fit the mold of a skinny Barbie doll type, as she has a curvy body. Rather than shying away from her curves and dressing in clothes that hide them, she has embraced her body wearing form-fitting clothing. As a result, the once relatively unknown girl is now one of the most sought-after women in the world today. You have to give her credit, despite being so obvious to see, she took advantage of the easily observable reaction men would give to this type of body/style/appearance.

Since she has become the sex symbol she is today, she has worked on her body through both working out and dieting to take it to another level, but she didn't start there.

Dressing for four body type tips:

1. **Thin**
   Since thin women typically have more outfit choices, it's important to stay on track. Don't try to be too fashion-forward or dress in something boring that may be nice but doesn't stand out.

   You can get away with larger style clothing and more fashionable items. While this will still attract men, the universal outfit tips above apply to thin girls, as well. As you will see in the examples below, an oversized fashionable shirt may look good (left), but the fashionable oversized dress on the right looks terrible. Wearing anything oversized, regardless of its being in fashion or not should be judged on an item-by-item basis.

2. Average

This woman isn't skinny thin, though she isn't thick; she's normal and proportionate. As a result, there's a range of outfit choices for her, and she should use the same approach as the thin woman. Below are examples of how a fashionable oversized dress looks when compared to a more fitted dress. Men will feel drawn to the form-fitting one; they won't appreciate the oversized one, regardless of the fashion sense, designer name, or cost.

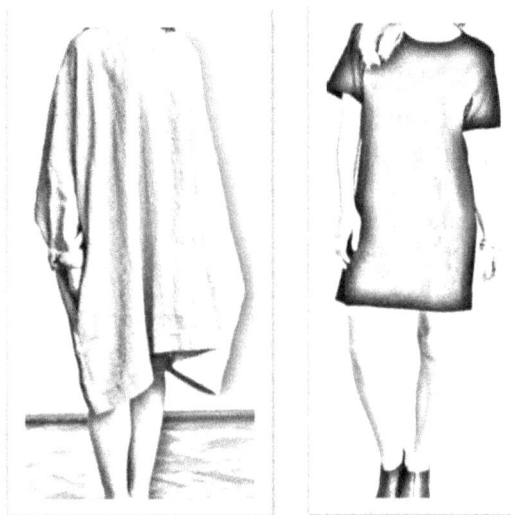

3. Full-figured

Being a little heavier can create challenges and limit options for clothing. The reason for this is most retailers produce in mass quantities at sizes that are most common. These women are well-proportioned, just a little heavier. It's also fairly common for a woman to have a small waist and big butt, the pear shape. There's also the apple shape, which is women who are rounder through the middle.

For the slightly heavier woman, play off your curves. Don't try to hide them with oversized clothing; instead, embrace them following the universal outfit tips above. Specifically, you should incorporate a nice skirt or dress with an elastic waistband that flairs out beneath it, or if the waistband isn't tight enough, add a belt. These are commonly known as fit and flare (fit around the waist, flare beneath). It will make your waist look smaller and lay nicely over your body. It will also leave enough to the man's imagination to keep his interest. Below are a couple of examples of the waist band skirts that should become a staple for your style.

4. Plus size

The options to find clothes for plus size women have improved over the years since there's such a demand for them. This is not something to be self-conscious about; you must embrace it.

This woman should accessorize like no other. This is covered in the next style point and will help you enjoy putting together an outfit. She should also follow the same steps as the thick woman, use a skirt or dress with an elastic waistband, avoid oversized clothes and follow the outline provided earlier in this chapter on color selection. Confidence and how you wear an outfit plays a significant role in how the outfit appears on you. Below are examples of styles you can wear to dress casually, for a night out, and a formal event.

For comparison purposes:

Below is an example of a button-down shirt with the following differences. The one on the left is more form-fitting, the one on right is oversized, the one on left is tucked in, the one on right is untucked, and there are two different body types. This is a very clear picture of how what you wear can either make you look attractive and highlight your positive features rather than looking unkempt. The outfits and how you wear the outfits make all the difference. Read on to learn how to pick the right outfits and colors and how to wear them to look your best.

STYLE POINT #4—SHOWING OFF YOUR BEST FEATURES

Great eyes
To bring out the color in your eyes, wear a shirt that closely matches your eye color. It will make your eyes stand out and catch others' attention.

Great legs
Rule number 1 is, of course, to make sure they're freshly shaved, especially if wearing a dress or shorts. If you have great legs, don't be afraid to show them off wearing tighter pants and shorter dresses or shirts to accentuate them.

Great smile
Outside of making sure they're always clean and white, smile! Smiling is the easiest way to show friendliness and personality.

Great breasts
Having great breasts is challenging for many women. Some show off too much, while others keep them completely concealed. Leaving something to the imagination garners better and more attention. For this reason, show off a little cleavage or skin but not enough to feel embarrassed or uncomfortable if you ran into a relative.

Great butt
Resist the temptation of showing off too much. Wearing short shorts shows off plenty; booty shorts are sure to attract attention from men you may not be interested in. Wearing tight pants, shorts, skirts, and dresses will show off your entire body, especially the butt without being offensive or obvious.

Great arms
Great arms are often overlooked and underappreciated. Many take a woman's arms for granted and, typically, only get noticed if they're out of shape and flabby. If you have nicely toned arms, wear sleeveless tops or dresses without hesitation.

STYLE POINT #5 ACCESSORIZING IS STYLE

Accessories reflect your personality in a tasteful, yet fun manner. Examples of this include bracelets, rings, and necklaces with different gem stones, colors, designs, or even messages. Great places to go for accessories include J. Crew, Express, Target, and Nordstrom. Vintage shops and flea markets are also cool spots to find unique pieces, too. You may find you can get unique pieces at most stores, though you must identify a cool style, not just simply pick something to be different.

Jewelry
Some women wear the same earrings, necklace, or bracelet(s), every day because they like those pieces and are comfortable wearing them. That's fine if you're not in the dating world. With the number of options with rings, bracelets, necklaces, and earrings, you must use these as opportunities to differentiate yourself.

Have fun choosing unique jewelry but don't go overboard with too many or too odd pieces; you're still looking to attract good attention, not odd or bad attention. Part of the reason for choosing unique pieces is that they're more likely to lead to a conversation with a man. Don't lose sight of this. Examples of this include a fashionable ring as pictured below of a snake, the group of multiple bracelets used as one piece, and the unique bracelet with a mixture of patterns and stones.

STYLE POINT #6 – HIGH HEELS

Some women live by the saying the higher the heel, the closer to God!

There aren't as many pitfalls in terms of attracting guys in terms of shoes. Guys, of course, like heels. Many women do too because it provides a lift-up of their butt and makes their legs look thinner. High heels provide a way to stand out. They also give you an opportunity to show your style. Examples, as shown below, include stones, studs, animal patterns, different buckles, heel design, and overall design. While it may be impractical to wear them at all times, wear a pair when you go out and bring a pair of flats or sandals in your bag to change into later.

Many women look at shoes to express themselves, and it seems the crazier and more unique the shoe, the better. Men are notorious for not noticing much (examples include if a woman gets a haircut and chops four inches off), but he will notice you in a pair of heels that stand out.

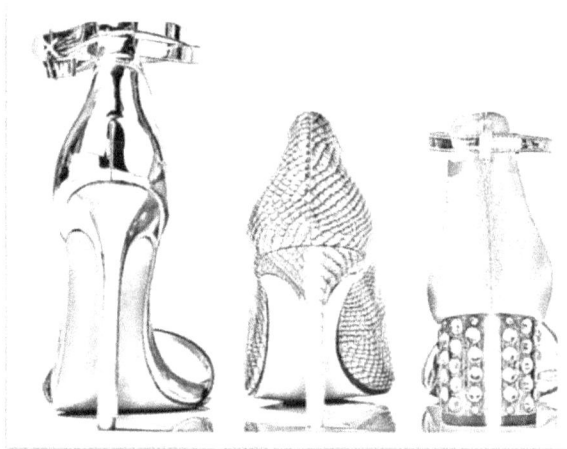

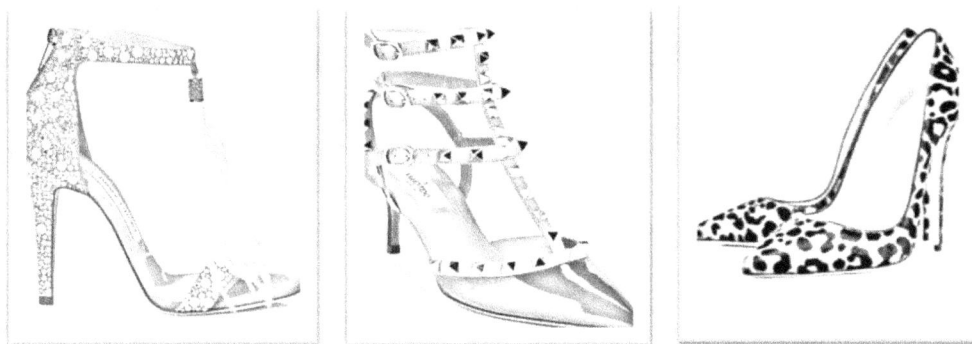

High heels are not the most comfortable shoe. In fact, most are uncomfortable. As a man, I can't imagine having to squeeze into a pair of tight heels and attempt to walk in them.

However, men and women both wear clothing and do things that aren't the most comfortable to improve their looks. High heels are no different, they can drastically improve a woman's appeal. There are concerns regarding the negative impact heels can have on your body as illustrated below. This book is to get men to want you, not to provide medical advice.

In the illustration to the left, the woman on the right wearing heels has her legs looking more toned from her calves to her thighs, and the heels lift her butt to make it look more toned as well. The example on the right shows how impactful the difference is between wearing flats and heels when looking directly at a woman as well. Some would argue it makes you look thinner in addition to being more toned.

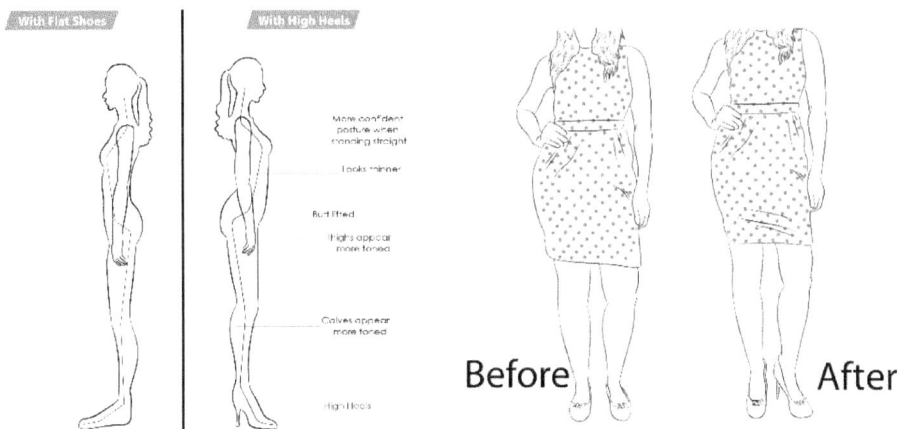

Now that you have an easy to understand outline with the six style points detailed for you, you can start immediately. It must be fun for you, whether you're coming into your own style or improving your current style, enjoyment must be a priority. The more enjoyable it is for you to be the best you, the better you'll look and feel. A byproduct of improving your appearance and self-esteem will be women complimenting you in addition to the men now wanting you.

CHAPTER 7:
DEVELOPING THE "IT" FACTOR OR X FACTOR (CREATING AN AURA)

"Whatever he has, I want it."

—Samantha from the show, Sex and the City

The "It" factor is how someone makes you feel when you're around them, whether it be butterflies, a giddy feeling of enthusiasm, or excitement being in their presence.

We've all experienced being out in public where there's a person who seems to light up the room. This same person gains a lot of attention from the opposite sex. It's almost as though he has a magnet drawing people closer in both attention and physical movement. The most powerful part of them lighting up the room is they do it with grace, not with words or obnoxiousness. This is a person who has an aura. You want this.

The goal is to walk in a room and compel others to notice you and to sense your *presence*. You've arrived. Heads will turn toward you, people will smile, and others will come to be around you.

To have an aura, you must develop a presence. Yes develop, as some must create it. You're about to learn how.

If you want people to give you positive attention, begin with holding your shoulders back and smiling. Good posture gives your appearance one of power and confidence. By smiling, anyone who looks at you and makes eye contact will naturally smile back.

Before the interaction in person, you must plan ahead using these four steps to continue your quest to have the "It" factor.

1. Dress in an outfit you feel confident shows you at your best.
2. Make sure your hygiene is up to par (teeth brushed, properly groomed, recently showered).
3. Do your hair.
4. Look at yourself in a mirror, smile, and feel good.

Once the four steps prior to going out in public are complete and you get to your destination, follow these seven steps:

1. Walk in with a smile on your face.
2. Smile often to anyone you notice looking at you on either side (eye contact is crucial, so make it).
3. Keep your shoulders held back with your head directly above your shoulders in a straight line.
4. Walk confidently.
5. Greet anyone you know and don't know with a simple "Hello" and smile.
6. Create small talk if the opportunity arises to compliment them on their outfit or about how nice the place is.
7. Wave to others that may be looking at you to ease the attention. They're likely to wave back, which will increase your confidence further.

The perception for anyone who sees you enter the room is you're a very popular person, which increases your value to others who don't know you. It will lead to more men wanting your attention than if you simply walked in and kept to yourself.

CHAPTER 8:
HOW TO BE CHARMING

"The more a man feels as though you're impressed by him, the more attracted he'll be to you."

—Michael Anthony

What is charm? Is it likeability, popularity, or both? Many have difficulty trying to describe it. In fact, chances are you may have wondered how so many like some people, while others aren't as well-liked. The person who's well-liked is charming and interesting. The other tends to be reserved and boring.

As stated in the book *How to Marry a Multi-Millionaire: The Ultimate Guide to High Net Worth Dating*, "Being charming, sexy, and flirtatious is an important tool for getting what you want from another person." [1]

The person who has "it" has charm. Charm gives you an aura, which you can create by mixing the proper ingredients. Many who are charming have similar traits such as being a good listener, speaking eloquently, and having strong mannerisms and gestures. Charm is not one trait alone. It's a mixture of many things, each of which plays an important role in becoming charming. The goal of this chapter is to prepare you with the necessary tools to charm anyone, from the man who already likes you to the man paying you little to no attention.

The book *The Power of Charm* by Brian Tracy and Ron Arden says "Women love men who are charming. They want to be with them constantly. To be charming, you have to understand how they think and feel." Women feel attracted to charming people, and men are as well.

Below are 10 actions to create charm immediately. These have played a paramount role in my life for relationships, additional sales, stronger friendships, new friendships, and most important to you, dating.

TEN ACTIONS TO CREATE CHARM IMMEDIATELY

The 1st Action—Confidence: Holding your shoulders back, wearing a nice outfit, being neatly groomed, smelling good, and smiling will give you the confidence needed to create a level of charm that will change your life. You'll learn more about each of these later in the book.

The 2nd Action—Maintaining Good Eye Contact: This is the most obvious way a person can tell you're paying attention to them. If you were to look away, they'll question whether you're paying attention or may even question you about what they just said. (We've all been there.) Looking away while they're talking is also a dead giveaway you feel distracted or aren't paying attention. It's simple, make eye contact, they don't have to know you're spacing out as long as you're looking into their eyes.

The 3rd Action—Shifting Your Eyes: To not come across as too intense, an eye shift is worth implementing. This is the simple act of shifting your gaze from one of their eyes to the other while listening to them talk. This will also seem more genuine, make them feel more comfortable, and will eliminate prolonged staring that can create discomfort.

The 4th Action—Smiling: Smiling to someone makes them feel more at ease with you and typically generates a smile in return. This will make both parties feel better and is the first step to being on the same page. When you smile, practice having your top row of teeth showing only. Having a smile with both your top and bottom rows of teeth showing can come across as a little over the top. When you smile, do it in a genuine manner; a fake smile is easy to spot.

The 5th Action—Nodding Your Head: Use the head nod to show affirmation of your agreement about the topic. The head nod also shows you're engaged in the conversation and not distracted.

The 6th Action—Positive Body Language: Position your entire body facing the person you're talking with. Be sure to keep a fair distance; sitting and standing distance should be roughly two feet apart to avoid invading their personal space. By having your body facing them shows you're giving them your undivided attention with your body language.

The 7th Action—Avoid Negative Body Language: While sitting, avoid having your legs crossed and having your knee on your top leg point away from the other person. Also, avoid having your face and body pointing in opposite directions. While standing, be sure to keep your arms at your sides because crossing them will look as though you're closed off and avoid having your hands behind your back or in your pockets. You also should keep your distance in a conversation.

 If you're in someone's personal space, they'll find you too abrasive and not charming at all. If someone feels you're too close for comfort, they'll tilt their head back away from your direction and may either step back or create a barrier with their arm between the two of you.

The 8th Action—Verbal Reassurances: The following phrases are great examples of verbal reassurances since they develop rapport, while not standing firm in agreement with their statement or beliefs. Examples include "Interesting," "That makes sense," "I understand," "Got it," "I see," and "Seriously?"

The 9th Action—Vocal Reassurances: These actions are little noises that don't say anything, although they mean a lot to the person talking. You'll notice that good, active listeners always make little noises like "Uh-huh," "Aah," and "Mmhmmm," or other assorted sounds. These are what we like to call "vocal reassurances." [2] These are clear indicators you're in tune with their conversation.

The 10th Action—Tilting Your Head: Tilting your head to either side gives the appearance you're taking in the conversation with deep thought and attention. Though a slight tilt of your head seems like such a small detail (which it is), it's vital to your success. Think of a time when you watched a movie, and you sympathized with a character. You most likely tilted your head to show sympathy. We have a tilt for sympathy when they show they need it. The head tilt is also useful when there's an engaging story, a funny joke, etc. The goal of the head tilt is to create an in-depth connection.

Dr. Albert Mehrabian of UCLA conducted a seminal study of communication and concluded that 55 percent of the message you send in a face-to-face conversation is through your body language, 38 percent in the way the words are spoken (paralinguistic), while the words themselves represent only 7 percent. [3] Author Ray Birdwhistell used the word "kinesics" in the title of his 1970 book *Kinesics and Context: Essays on Body Motion Communication* to describe and explain the movement of the human body when it uses all its senses. This was a groundbreaking observation by Birdwhistell, and it's one of the bases of all the research that has been and is still being performed on nonverbal communication, i.e. body language. [4]

Body language is the single most powerful communication channel. Communication research has demonstrated repeatedly that when body language and the content of communication are ambiguous, people will *always* believe body language *over* words. [5]

It's amazing how well you can dissect a person or a relationship without hearing them talk. Here's an exercise for you to do. While out to eat, look around the room and make judgments about couples you see eating together. Judging only their body language, you should be able to tell if they're on good terms, in a poor mood, fighting, or if one has little to no interest in the other. From the tips listed previously, you now have unbelievable social identification power in your hands. However, it's only useful if you use it.

You should be able to identify the level of interest a person has in you quickly. Identifying their interest allows you to decide whether their interest in you matches your interest in them. Then, you can decide whether he's a good fit or someone you're interested in.

Last and most important, one of the easiest ways to charm a man, or any person for that matter, is by finding mutual interests and what he's passionate about. With online dating profiles and profiles on dating apps, your already have an advantage because you can simply view his profile and read the detailed information he provided about himself and look at his pictures for more insight.

If you'd like to expand further, you search online for their name, phone number, or email address to see what comes up. If the site already links to Facebook, you should have more than enough ammunition to find mutual interests.

You can use this information to get a competitive edge over others vying for a man's attention because you'll have the leg up on his interests, dislikes, etc. Having this information is key because you can then mold your conversations with him to common interests, such as your favorite band and your favorite food.

You should establish these common interests in a very smooth, covert way. You can't use this as a talking point to begin with, but rather something you can add to the conversation seamlessly. Below is a case study on examples of how women have successfully added these types of shared interests in a conversation online. Yes, you can be charming and form a connection online, too.

CASE STUDY

Woman: Do you by chance like sushi??
Man: Yes, I love sushi!
Woman: Nice, I was going to say there is a great place on Main Street that just opened up. It's a little pricey, but worth it. The quality and freshness is how I justify the price 😊
Man: Thanks, I am definitely going to have to check it out.
Woman: We may just get along after all, haha

Man: I am exhausted from work. Today felt like a Monday, luckily tomorrow is Friday though
Woman: It is Friday, so stay positive. I know it's easier said than done.
Man: One of the guy that works with me is so annoying.
Woman: There is a perfect solution for this – Drake on the iPod!
Man: Drake is the man. I saw him last year in Toronto!
Woman: I haven't seen him in concert yet, how was he?
Man: Awesome! I would definitely go again. When he comes in town next, I will line up tickets.
Woman: Just give me notice as I need to plan these things in advance 😊

Both case study samples are from a longer conversation. However, as you can see above, the connection established happened very quickly without coming across as out of place. This is an easy way to establish a connection, when there's a connection but not yet discovered. Do not lie or mislead. This is meant to help identify whether the two of you click after finding a common interest.

There's a fine line between having things in common and coming off as a stalker. You don't want to creep him out by being too coincidental; he'll feel uncomfortable and uneasy. You don't want to admit to looking him up initially either; that may not go over well. After the fact, when you've bonded, you can tell him since he most likely tried looking you up, too!

CHAPTER 9:
HOW TO SHOW YOUR SENSE OF HUMOR

"Trying to be funny is different from being funny."

—Unknown

Everyone has a sense of humor. It's rare to find someone who is in sync with you completely. However, since you're looking to find a man who isn't identical to you, this is a good thing.

In showing your sense of humor, you must be cautious not to be offensive to others. If you're being malicious or mean, it won't matter what you say, it will create awkwardness and not go over well. See the outlined humors below for insights in the types of humors and remember people like to be laughed with not laughed at.

FIVE TYPES OF HUMORS OUTLINED

1. Jokes

    A casual joke is acceptable. Going into a routine with more than one joke can come across as odd and not genuine. Jokes are for friends and your younger years, not dating.

2. Laughing at yourself

    Laughing at yourself can show your sense of humor and ability not to take yourself too seriously. Be cautious not to go overboard. A simple observation or innocent joke at your expense is acceptable but nothing more. You want him to like you, not highlight or point out your negative features.

3. Laughing to make someone feel better

    If someone is telling a story is it OK to laugh, despite not thinking it's funny. By doing it, you're creating rapport and making them feel good.

4. Laughing at your peers

At a time when sensitivity is at all-time high, laughing at someone, even friends, can seem as if you're making fun of them or bullying them. Know your audience. Don't assume the person can take a joke; many can't. And never laugh at someone you don't know.

5. Laughing at something

This is the best way to show your sense of humor. Laughing at something with others, which doesn't hurt, bother, or offend anyone else is innocent and enjoyable.

It's safe to say you see yourself using each of these types of humor regularly. To show your sense of humor, knowing your audience is important. The reason why is because not everyone has the same taste in humor. Some may find something hilarious, while others may be very offended.

However, to show your sense of humor, tread lightly by learning more about how the man thinks and what he finds humor in. You can do this with innocent comments to see if he takes the bait by also commenting. If he doesn't take the bait, and you can't gain insight into what would be safe, tread cautiously until an opportunity presents itself. If he does take the bait and you can determine what he finds funny, you should then act on it by citing real experiences you've had, funny shows or movies you've watched, or ask him his favorite show or movie.

Showing your sense of humor has as much to do with comfort and the right audience as the words and messaging. You can't be the answer to someone's prayers unless you know what they're praying for.

CHAPTER 10:
HOW TO CREATE CONFIDENCE

"Confidence is silent. Insecurities are loud."

—Popular saying

$$\text{CONFIDENCE} = \frac{\text{Mental Clarity Defined}}{\text{Physical Clarity Action}}$$

Confidence is momentum. Momentum is multiple reassurances or successes in a row. Once someone has multiple reassurances, successes, or compliments in a row, they feel better. Their feeling better leads to an increase in their confidence.

Creating confidence is easier than creating momentum. It takes more time and continual successes to create momentum. In contrast, you can create confidence very quickly, as you will see below. Once you create confidence, you'll develop momentum naturally, which increases your confidence further.

To create confidence, you must identify what will make you confident. If you don't know, you must think back to times when you felt good and identify what was responsible for those feelings. This require deep thought to get the mental clarity required to move forward.

For different people, there are different items. Some want to look their best, and when they're told they look good, they're confident. Some think they must prove it to themselves through physical actions that result in success to be confident. While others simply just want to feel good about themselves, and that leads them to being confident.

Your confidence processes in your mind through your actions and appearance. Actions that lead to success are the most surefire ways to increase your confidence in your ability. For more in-depth examination, read the "Creating Charm" chapter. Your appearance can give you confidence in your physical appearance and mental state. Others you'll meet will notice this, too. Enhancing your appearance is one of the quickest—if not the easiest—ways to increase your confidence. Dressing in nice, fashionable clothes, being freshly groomed, and smelling nice can transform your physical appearance instantly.

If you want to dramatically increase your confidence, tan a few times and go to the gym on a regular basis. The reasons for going to the gym are not to become a fitness model but to be in better shape, mentally and physically. Simply going to the gym will increase your confidence, regardless of the weight you may lift or exercises you may do but because you'll feel healthier and be in overall better shape.

Tanning is one of the quickest transformations you can make to your physical appearance. You feel healthier, and it's widely accepted that people look better in the summer when they're tan. Conventional and spray tans are both great options if you don't look orange. These examples are just a few of the most effective ways to create a change in your confidence in the quickest amount of time.

As the book *The Rules: Time-Tested Secrets for Capturing the Heart of Mr. Right* by Ellen Fein and Sherrie Schneider states, "Look your best! The better you look, the better you will feel and the more desirable you will become." [6]

Translation: As you enhance your appearance, your confidence will increase from the attention you'll receive from others, and that attention will yield more attention and create momentum for your confidence.

It's important to remember, that going to the gym one time will not result in a six-pack, toned body, or flat stomach for that matter. However, the direct effect on your mindset, combined with the new activity for your muscles is sure to energize you and increase your confidence immediately. The most important part is the invaluable help it will give your mindset.

You should strive to be the confident woman who walks in without any hesitancy or insecurities on display. You have every reason to feel confident if you implement the strategies given to you to enhance your appearance, improve your style, be charming and have the "it" factor.

REAL LIFE EXAMPLE

While visiting friends in Vegas, I convinced a few friends to drive to Los Angeles to check out an LA Lakers basketball game. We arrived about 15 minutes late and I lucked into some great seats—front row, actually! The only better seats in the gym were courtside. About 20 minutes into the game, the two courtside seats directly in front of me, roughly five feet away, were still empty. As luck would have it, Adam Sandler and Steven Spielberg came in and sat directly in front of me! As you might imagine, I was in disbelief. I immediately decided to use the surroundings to my advantage. Hell, everyone in LA is someone, right? I looked over and saw Adam Levine, the lead singer for Maroon 5 courtside, and not far from him was actor Kevin James, actor David Arquette, model Diane Cannon, and the list goes on.

It was clear this was a once-in-a-lifetime experience, and I told myself I belonged there. Though guards were everywhere, ranging from Staples Center personnel to personal security guards, I acted like I not only owned the place; I acted like I belonged. As I took in the scene courtside, talking to celebrities, I had a couple of strangers reach out to shake my hand. After the game, I stayed behind and hung out with the players' families and friends, as well as the actual players themselves. No one questioned who I was or if I was allowed there because I didn't let the opportunity come up.

I am willing to bet accomplishing this at a Lakers game is a bit more difficult than what you might encounter online. It all starts with taking that chance. You miss every shot you don't take.

Now, go own the dating world as if you belong.

THE FUNDAMENTALS OF ONLINE DATING DEFINED

CHAPTER 11:

WHY ONLINE DATING IS FAR SUPERIOR TO ANY DATING OR MATCHMAKING SERVICE

"Being busy is a form of laziness – lazy thinking and indiscriminate action."

– Timothy Ferriss, author of *The 4-Hour Workweek*

It must be understood why people hire matchmaking or dating services. The common answer is that they have a hectic schedule and do not have "time." The truth behind this answer is that the woman or man is being lazy and is hoping for everything to fall into place with as little inconvenience and work as possible.

You see, when a woman signs up for a dating or matchmaking service, she is at an immediate disadvantage. She is placing her trust in a service that only knows her based upon his answers to a questionnaire or what she is able to relay to them in their brief meetings. She is trusting a stranger to make judgments on her behalf. This is clearly concerning.

Think about it: the dating service or matchmaker only knows to search for what you tell them to search for. The reality is that you sometimes don't know exactly what you want, and what is attractive to you can vary based on the day or your mood. These services cannot learn everything about you in a quick phone conversation or a sit-down meeting. And let's be honest, who knows you better than you?

Because you know your likes and dislikes better than anyone else, it makes far more sense to join an online dating site or app without these services. The setup is already favorable for you as you can access the sites around your hectic schedule to save time and maximize efficiency. Now that everything has gone mobile, you can access it on your phone at any time, so time is on your side.

By joining an online dating site and using dating apps, you are 100% in control of who you talk to and when. You can decide if you are attracted to something or someone outside of what you may have written down on paper. Despite being attracted to clean cut guys, you may be interested in a bad boy at a certain day or time. Frankly, the **biggest** problem with hiring a matchmaking service is **you are not in control**.

Matchmaking services promise a happily ever after. They work towards a commitment and ring to be put on your hand as soon as possible. Your intention may not be to "settle" down with just anyone. Settling implies taking less than you want and we don't agree with this approach, nor should you.

The divorce rate is so high because of this mindset.

It is natural for everything to be exciting when you first start hanging out with someone. Eventually, the honeymoon phase fades.

BIOLOGICAL CLOCK FACTOR

Despite the biological clock ticking for women who do not want to have kids after 35, you must still prioritize the right man and the right time. If not, you are simply rushing something for short term happiness, which can lead to a difficult forever.

These dating and matchmaking services brag about their conversion rate. However, the rate they publicize is typically based on their members eventually *dating* whom they set them up with. *They do not publish the break up and divorce rate.* That's because it would not be good for business!

High-end dating services are the most obviously flawed. The foundation is based on a man or woman landing a wealthy match. Perfect, let's allow some money-grubbing person to search you out for your money, not for being the right person at the right time. This is very disappointing.

Just imagine if the person who is on the high-end dating service is simply looking to use you for financial gain, where you may be sincere in your interest. As a result, you commit only to find out someone is using you down the road. It's possible it could be after you have a whirlwind romance and marry quickly.

Then what happens? Divorce, of course. This is the problem. Everyone likes the idea of being married more than the reality of being committed through marriage to another person for the rest of their life. See the statistics below to confirm that statement.

Percentages of Divorces [7]

Age at time of marriage	Women	Men
Under 20 years old	27.6%	11.7%
20-24 years old	36.6%	38.8%
25-29 years old	16.4%	22.3%
30-34 years old	8.5%	11.6%
35-39 years old	5.1%	6.5%

Percentage of first marriages ending in divorce: 41%
Percentage of second marriages ending in divorce: 60%
Percentage of third marriages ending in divorce: 73% [8]

The real question is: If you're going to be married for the rest of your life, why rush it?

As I conducted my research, I couldn't help but see the irony that the matchmaking and dating service consultants helping others find true love are either single or divorced.

CHAPTER 12:
UNIVERSAL DATING TIPS DEFINED

"Creating a universal understanding is like being given a cheat sheet for the game of life."

—Michael Anthony

Learning the "Universal Dating Tips" will improve your success in navigating and using online dating sites and dating apps. By incorporating the tips into your actions, you can expect the online scene to appear simplified and easy to navigate. This will put you in the best position to have men seek you out and get men to want you.

TOP 18 UNIVERSAL DATING TIPS

1. Create a quick default search. This will save your settings for your main search, including specifics such as age, distance from a ZIP code, interests, etc.

2. Create more detailed searches. Many sites and some apps will allow you to set up multiple searches you can save. Take advantage of this. For example, rather than setting up a search for 18- to 35-year-olds, expand this into searches for 18 to 21, 22 to 25, 26 to 30, and 31 to 35 years old. Having other searches set as additional defaults eliminates the need to change your search criteria repeatedly and helps you be in tune with new sign-ups.

3. Edit your custom search options. Only list or mark the deal breaker items. The options are many: marital status, education, height, weight, location, language, ethnicities, kids, drinking, smoking, salary, occupation, astrological sign, and pets, though you must step back and determine if some of those items are not complete deal breakers if he has many of the other characteristics you want. The goal is not to eliminate someone before checking out his profile. I would suggest creating a top four and marking the others "no preference" to keep your options open. The more specific you are, the fewer matches and results you'll get. Be vague, then evaluate.

4. Decide whether you'd like to activate the reverse and the mutual match features. This gives men the option to receive alerts about your profile if you have similar likes and characteristics as they do.

5. Decide whether you want your profile to appear private or not. If your profile is private, you can access profiles when you search, though others won't see you unless you contact them. This is a great option if you're hesitant and don't want to be seen on an online dating site or app just yet.

6. Identify the option to hide your profile so that others can't see you unless you initiate contact (stealth mode).

7. Decide whether you want to activate the "online now" status. If you do activate it, you can use instant messaging features to contact others if they're also online. You can also search specifically for men who are online.

8. Some sites offer daily notifications such as the "Daily 5 Results," which is a daily matching feature. Though the titles vary, they're all identical. You can select "yes" or "no" if you're interested in a person the site has paired you with. If you choose "yes," the man will receive an email about your interest, and he'll have the opportunity to respond.

9. Identify the options and account settings. This is very useful to block anyone you don't want to contact you.

10. Make notes of past conversations or take screenshots if anything is important to know. **Note:** Be careful doing this; there's always the chance someone will get their hands on it.

11. Don't give out too much information (including your full name) when chatting online. There's little good that can come from giving your full name or work email address; they can research you with that information.

12. Be cautious when adding any men from an online dating site or app to a social networking site. A lot of your personal information is available on the social networking site, and they can access your network of friends and family.

13. Never ask a man out on a date. If you are interested in hanging out, joke around and make it more casual, such as hanging out. Once a man feels he is being asked out on a date, he may freak out as his mind can gravitate towards the c level, most are so scared of: commitment.

14. Send all email correspondence and search results to a personal email account, not a business one.

15. Be 100 percent truthful in your profile description. This includes your body type, height, and weight. Your goal is to meet the person, and if you're lying, you're wasting your time and theirs.

16. Never list any range for the salary field. Regardless of whether your salary is high or low, it's not necessary and won't help, as the man will judge you on this either way.

17. Be prepared to tell someone why you're better than most of the other women on the site. This shouldn't be a long list, but something you can rattle off the top of your head quickly. Base the list on what you have to offer outside of looks.

18. Don't hesitate to pay for premium member benefits. Start with the shortest paid option to see whether the results justify it. If you notice results, keep it.

Now that you have read and understand the reasoning behind the Top 18 Universal Dating Tips, you can use this information to enhance your success on dating sites and dating apps. This information is priceless in terms of streamlining the process for you. As you incorporate this knowledge, you can expect your success to follow.

CHAPTER 13:
TOP THREE ONLINE DATING SITES ANALYZED

"Directions were meant to take the guesswork of getting where you want to go. If you have directions, use them."

—Joseph Zachary

This chapter is a short cut to choosing the right dating sites and apps to put you in the best position as possible to find eligible men.

Online dating is different from traditional dating so you must understand that your past dating successes or failures don't translate to online success or failure.

They key to succeeding in online dating and on dating apps is to establish a universal map to produce results. At that point, you'll discover how online dating can be much easier than traditional dating. Before you get there, you first must identify which sites best align with your wants and needs.

Below is a breakdown of the most popular online dating sites and apps for you to review. Ultimately, you must determine which ones fit what you're looking for.

WWW.MATCH.COM

- Founded in 1995, helped pioneer the online dating industry
- More than 20 million users
- 49% to 51% men-to-women ratio

Match.com is one of if not *the* most popular dating site today in terms of quality. Match.com has made acquisitions of competitors in the past to further strengthen its customer base. It's a dominant player in today's online dating world and control Chemistry.com, BlackPeopleMeet.com, OurTime.com (for the 50+ crowd), SingleParentsMeet.com, Christian Dating through LoveAndSeek.com and Personals.com among others.

While Match.com has had notable successes in the dating world, the percentages favor those looking to date. Though some hope to find "the one," the odds are not in favor of this, so joining Match, where the selection is greatest, can yield the most options for you. Match.com is a step above PlentyOfFish.com in quality because there's a fee associated with membership. The members on Match are typically younger in comparison to the members at eHarmony.com.

Site Specific Tips

- You can track and reset the number of times men view your profile.
- The site will keep a running tally for you regarding the number of winks and emails sent and received.
- With the Daily 5, Match will connect you with five people you may be interested in.
- You simply click interested or not on each of the Daily 5 prospects, and they will receive notifications only if you're interested. If it's a match, they connect you two.
- Typically, there's a trial period. Take advantage of this so you can decide, based on the prospects, if it's the right site for you to invest your time in.

WWW.EHARMONY.COM

- 33 million members in the US
- In nearly 200 countries around the world
- Harris Interactive states an average of 542 eHarmony members in the United States marry every day.

eHarmony is a site focused on creating long-term, lasting relationships. The site requires members to complete a questionnaire totaling more than 400 questions for compatibility. The site requires its members to complete many steps to ensure the members are, in fact, serious about finding "love." This website is mostly for older users. According to Quantcast, 71 percent of users are women. This could be a negative for women except the men that are on eHarmony tend to be more serious.

After completing the profile and the questionnaire, members can't search the site for men. eHarmony provides matches to you via email. This takes the control out of the member's hand, which isn't good for you since it imposes limitations to your search capabilities and how many men you can contact. This is good for members looking for serious compatibility. The matches provided to you are based on the answers you gave on the questionnaire as well as the information you provided regarding what you're looking for. eHarmony matches that information with men who seem compatible with you based on their answers on the questionnaire and criteria such as age and other specifics.

Site Specific Tips

- eHarmony provides hints on completing your profile assessment. Mainly, the hints are to help you to give details.
- Depending on your membership level, you might have the option to have your ID verified for protection or a deeper analysis of your personality; you might request photos from matches, see who has viewed your profile, and send/receive communication requests.

- Members can control preferences on potential matches sent to them based on their distance from your ZIP code; whether you're interested in someone who drinks, smokes, or has kids; religious preferences; and education.
- eHarmony basically controls the access to its members. It isn't as open as its competitors, which most likely helps its members find someone on an emotional level.
- Most people online want to search and view their potential matches' pictures. eHarmony focuses more on connecting on an emotional level.
- I recommend going through a free trial period so you can decide, based on the prospects, whether this site fits what you're looking for.

WWW.PLENTYOFFISH.COM

- More than 4 million people using it daily
- 70,000 new sign-ups per day
- Over 10 billion page views every month

Plenty of Fish is a free dating website and app. The popular site is one of the easiest to navigate. The site is open to everyone, so there are people from all walks of life—from the best of the best to the worst of the worst. The quality prospects may mix with a large quantity of those who don't have the qualities you want. Often, you will see the same people on other dating sites who are on Plenty of Fish. Don't let this deter you. This is one of if not the best site to meet men quickly for free.

The site offers a chemistry test and a test to discover your relationship needs. The site also offers a "Relationship Chemistry Predictor" questionnaire. As stated in the universal do's and don'ts sections, do not get too sentimental with details; your goal is to appeal to everyone. Then, you can decide whom to proceed with.

Site Specific Tips

- At the bottom of each profile there's a number next to "favorites." The higher this number is, the more likely the prospect has been on the site for a long time and is not a desirable prospect for you.
- You can check out who has viewed your profile from your homepage.
- You can also make your profile private and access additional features such as specifics on profile views so that no one can see whether you viewed their profile.
- It's possible to see someone's last log in. This lets you know whether they're an "active" member. If they haven't been online for a while, you know they're inactive, and you can save yourself the time of contacting them.
- This site is also accessible as POF or www.POF.com.

IN CLOSING

Now that you have the universal map you need to succeed in selecting the right sites, navigate around them, perform searches, design your profile, and identify good and bad prospects and more, you now simply must act.

CHAPTER 14:
TOP MOBILE DATING APPS ANALYZED

"The only advice I can give you is to expect anything you type or send from your phone to be viewed by everyone you don't want to see it."

—A father handing his son his first cell phone

New apps and online dating sites are being created daily. Many will come, and most will go. The strategies, insights and analysis provided within this book are universal. They have stood the test of time and are currently working today.

Just as traditional dating has shifted online due to the convenience and efficiency needed for our hectic lifestyles, mobile dating has taken the reins from online dating. People can check their phone throughout the day, receive notifications in real time and talk anytime using the phone, which is typically nearby.

With our attention spans at an all-time low and expectations of getting what we want now, the mobile dating market through apps have taken the dating market by storm.

The larger online sites have taken notice and have their own apps, too. A smart phone is all you need to start online dating today. At the tips of your fingertips is literally thousands of different men on display for you to check out.

To help you gain a better understanding on the best apps to use, here are 15 general tips:

15 GENERAL TIPS FOR APPS

1. When viewing photos or profiles, you simply swipe your finger across and it directs you to the next photo/profile. Despite the appearance that pictures are all that's shown, most apps, as with actual dating sites have profiles with information such as age, height, weight, about me section, headline, etc.

2. Do not merge your dating site with your Facebook account.

3. If you have merged your account with Facebook, avoid logging in through your Facebook account. These are recipes for disaster because your personal information, friend lists, work info, etc. are there for everyone to see.

4. Despite merging your Facebook account, showing you've been "verified," it's not worth it.

5. In contrast, a man who has his account merged is great because you a) know he's real and b) can do some research on him to get more information

6. Don't bite on profiles that have only one photo if the site allows for more. Quantity in terms of information and photos is important for validation, while not sacrificing your quality expectations.

7. Use the settings to show whether someone is currently logged-in or online. This is the best type of person to reach out to because they're an active user. More important, if you're both online at the same time, it's very convenient for interacting.

8. Keep an eye on any "New Sign-Ups." If you're interested in a man who's new, you must act quickly before he's overwhelmed.

9. Adjust your settings and pay the fee if there is one to see who's viewing or has viewed you. This is important to see because, since they were intrigued enough to check out your profile, you can reach out to them after they view you. Check this regularly and quickly message anyone who has viewed your profile that you find promising.

10. In sales, the response time plays a key role in having conversion success. The same is true for online dating. You must be quick with your responses because the more time passes, the more options (distractions) he'll have. You must capitalize when interest is at its highest and he's still focused on you.

11. Set up a new email just for dating sites and apps. It's much easier to organize and reduces the possibility of mixing work with fun or revealing personal information.

12. Create a system for organizing the experience. It's easy to get overwhelmed and distracted since there's so much to sort through. If you're organized, you can ensure you're not missing a man you may be interested in.

13. Attention spans are shorter than ever. For this reason, pictures and quick hit information are more important than ever before. So be sure to have your best pictures highlighted.

14. There's a time to be cheap and time not to. The features many apps offer to highlight your profile, see who has viewed your profile, and certain messaging capabilities are worth it. As a result, you will talk to more men, meet more men, and see higher quality men.

15. While online dating sites and some apps may be different with various features, the fundamental principles are the same for you to experience success in getting men to want you.

Now that you have the tips for all sites; below you'll find specific detailed information for different apps and insights to help you choose the right app for you, while increasing your odds, regardless of the dating app.

TINDER

This app has taken over. With its popularity at an all-time high, the number of members is continually increasing. The more members, the better for you. It's free to start and is very easy to navigate. Both parties must agree to "match," This eliminates a lot of the guesswork before talking. Below is a quick breakdown of features Tinder offers:

- Logs in with a phone number or Facebook.
- Uses swipe technology to view pictures and profiles.
- Can "Skip the line" and be the top profile for 30 minutes to get more matches.
  - Highly recommended; it will increase your exposure, interest, and odds of meeting men.
- Can "like" a profile, "super like," or discard it.
- For a fee, you can get Tinder Plus, which gives you unlimited likes, 1 free boost a month, and control of what others see about you. You can also choose who sees you, and you can customize your setting to show only to those you liked, etc.
- When you're a paying member, you can "rewind," to go back to a profile you mistakenly swiped too quickly. This is a great feature.
- Your main picture is the focus of your profile, though, beneath there's a location and various other information.
  - Neat features include the listed distance away from each other, which can prove beneficial, if interested, and both members have their location settings on. It allows them to see how feasible it is to hang out if they're already near one another.
  - Despite not having as much weight, a bio/about me section is still there, where you can write three or four sentences to help you stand out.
- Tinder allows you to link Instagram pictures and connect on Instagram.
  - Do this cautiously; many have personal information, including family photos, work photos, pictures with friends, etc. on Instagram.
- Can recommend a profile to a friend.
- Premium feature of "Passports Plus," which allows you to swipe around the world. This is great if you're traveling or may be traveling to an area soon.
- A paid membership offers additional features such as no ads.
  - Not showing your age
  - Not showing your location
  - Eliminating the annoying advertisements

ZOOSK

Zoosk started as a Facebook app in December 2007 and is now available in more than 25 languages and more than 80 countries. Zoosk can pull up your information from your social networking account to help create your profile if you decide to link it. Keep an eye on your settings and what you're sharing—with and without your permission. Once you start to receive messages, a popup appears that states "You must be a subscriber to send messages" If you choose to proceed, they have subscriptions ranging from monthly to three months at a time and six months at a time. This is a great strategy by Zoosk, since it allows you to send a message and receive one, and then you're hooked because you need to subscribe to send further messages. Before Tinder, Zoosk was dominant. Below is a quick summary of Zoosk:

- More than 35 million members
- A tutorial to make it more user-friendly, which is great for a new member
- Swipe to see profiles
- Room for messages and emojis under the profile picture (recommended)
- A "smart pick" option, which is a feature to match you and others
- Radar function to see who's nearby, based on your distance specifications (within 5, 10, 15, 20 miles, etc.)
- Messaging service to chat directly
- The ability to see who has viewed your profile and whether you viewed theirs
- Function to reply to emails sent by premium members
- Premium members with all-access
- Ads that generate revenue, annoying but a fact
- Credit called "coins."
- Options to get "coins" free:
  - Invite friends to join Zoosk
  - Become a fan of the Zoosk Facebook page
  - Install the Zoosk dating application on your iPhone
- Additional options using "coins"
  - Capability to go invisible (which can be good for privacy)
  - Can purchase "Boost Profile" to increase your profile views by having your profile highlighted and at the top of search results (the more people who see you the better for getting men to want you)
  - Delivery confirmation. Find out if the person has read your message
  - Special delivery. Make sure he sees your message before all the others
  - Send gifts (not recommended; this is not how you want to get his attention)

POF

POF, also known as Plenty Of Fish is the largest free site or app out there today, with more than 4 million people using it daily and more than 70,000 new members every day. As with anything in life that's free, it may not always yield the best quality, but the quantity is there. This translates into more than 1 billion messages per month. Below are some quick facts and pointers for using POF:

- Option to see whether the attraction is mutual by simply expressing your interest in a member with a single click
- Can hide your profile, which may be necessary at times
- Popups with tips and facts
  - An alarming one: "Income is the single biggest predictor of relationship failure and of relationships starting. Please select your income range."

- Can lead to lies and isn't a good way to start
- Add-ons for a better user experience. These include:
  - Upgrade to 1st look, which allows your profile to be at the top of search results. Puts your messages first in the line a man may receive. Great advantage for many to see you.
  - The Ultra-Match, a personalized service of the Top 50 matches
  - Top Prospect presented to you
  - Seeing who has viewed your profile (great feature; you can message them, since you clearly caught their attention to click on your profile).
  - As with all sites with a paid option, you pay less for the longer length of your commitment, for instance 12 months is less than six months, etc.
- Socials for singles to meet, a great opportunity since all the attendees are clearly single and ready to mingle.

OK CUPID

OK Cupid has recently attempted to differentiate itself from the other sites and not compete with the POF and Tinder markets. It's marketing the site as superior to its competitors by "getting to know the real you" through a more detailed questionnaire to know you on a deeper level. It has a proprietary algorithm that arranges matches and helps you find authentic connections based on common interests and answers from a questionnaire. While the approach makes sense, it's a less crowded space with only eHarmony and Match as similar competitors. Below is a condensed outline to get familiar with OK Cupid:

- Keep your personal information private, no signing in using Facebook unlike Tinder or Bumble
- Cumbersome questionnaire, but necessary to answer some of the questions to proceed
- Gain more insight into a potential partner based on the long quizzes and surveys
- Wide-ranging facts and questions between searches
- Quick match, a list of users with just their profile pictures
- Can also search based on who was online last, best match, mix (great feature; highly recommended)
- Percentage match feature allows a connection based on provided questions and information
  - Remember, less is more. The more info, the more vulnerable you are to fault-finding
- Ability to message people and "like" other profiles
- Must be a paid A-list member to see who likes you

BUMBLE

Bumble is a unique site because it has a feature unlike any other, which allows only the woman to send a message first. An ex-Tinder employee created Bumble to give the woman more control in the dating world. This is great for any man, as long as they receive messages. If you implement this book's tools and strategies to get men to want you, this is a great site. If you're still new to online dating, start with this app. It reduces the pressure of what to say, and you can get a behind-the-scenes view of what men say to crack the ice. However, this may also be a better site to use after you have confidence from interactions on other sites. Below are some details on the site:

- Most login through Facebook
- View profile using same swiping method as others
- Share a profile with a friend if you think they may be of interest or to get their thoughts
- A connection guide to assist with matches
- "Back Track" technology; can shake phone to go back if you swiped too soon
- Click on the name to show their location
- Option to share or block/report someone to an admin
- Additional services at a cost:
  - See who likes your profile
  - Access old matches
  - Unlimited "Extends" on previous matches or conversations
  - Time extension for them to send the first message (connection expires in 24 hours)
  - Reconnect with the person your connection fizzled out with if they don't send a message
  - "Bumble Boost," increases exposure to men searching profiles.

CLOVER

Clover is a different type of app because it reminds you on an old-school message board. The format allows members to post on a common board, though the members can take the conversation private. It offers a short free trial period of seven days and baits you with many great features to convince you to join. It has groups to help members identify the right fit for them. Below are some of the details you should know when using Clover:

- Log in can be through email or Facebook.
  - Use email; don't share your personal information with strangers
- Must enter your credit card info for free trial
  - After your trial period, membership starts immediately at $29.99 per month, though you can cancel at any time
- Allows members to see whether someone read their messages
- Quick interest options: a heart if you like them, an x if you don't have interest, or an option to message them directly
- Some of the many groups include:
  - Girls that want relationships
  - Nice guys
  - Socially awkward
  - Tall girls
  - Short guys
  - Pet lovers

MATCH

Match is the gold standard for online dating, specifically online. However, with its huge database online, many users also use the app. With a massive online presence, Match is a clear-cut winner. It has continually acquired competitors to assist with this growth. With such a powerful database, the launch of an app was an easy decision and a seamless transition. It has a large user base and requires members to pay, so the quality is arguably the best in terms of people. Most of the app features mirror the online site, though are still relevant and useful:

- Log in using your email
- Membership, most expensive for the shortest duration
- Options to save profiles
- Messages do not disappear
- Daily matches based on similar interests you and someone else state in a questionnaire
- Emojis such as a smile or wink
- Search options based on your current location, ZIP code, or distance
- Many photos, though profiles have depth with information
    - More about the man you may want to talk to, which makes conversation easier

SKOUT

Another site that has and will continually make a splash in the mobile market is Skout. Skout is a location-based app on your cell phone and has a presence in more than 100 countries in 14 languages. It identifies where you and the other users within their network are. For safety purposes, the app doesn't reveal the exact location, though it identifies the area. Users can see those who are near and view their profiles. If there's an interest, you can use the instant messaging feature to contact the other person. Skout prides itself on the users having complete safety. They also have a zero tolerance policy for bad or offensive behavior, which is a breath of fresh air for many. Below are more features on Skout:

- Holds itself to a higher standard with recommendations to members on meeting at public places.
- Allows users to see where those on their "friends list" on sites such as Facebook are
    - While it may not reveal the exact location, this is a prime opportunity for you to connect with someone
    - Could be a bad thing, so be cautious. If in a populated area, it may be easy to find the spot.
- Features to connect and share are wide-ranging:
    - Allows you to share photos
    - Can send messages through an instant messaging format
    - Option to send virtual gifts such as flowers (don't do it).
    - Can send notes if the person isn't online (think emails).

HINGE

Hinge is a dating app that connects you through friends. This eliminates the "stranger" aspect, which may appeal to you if you're looking for something serious. It could also be a bad fit if you aren't looking for awkwardness or potentially ruining friendships over a bad experience, date, or relationship. Join this site if you have a specific person you're interested in. If not, there are many pitfalls to justify it, unless you've exhausted other sites with no success and are looking for commitment.

- Add up to six photos
- Can add captions beneath photos
- iOS users can upload a video in lieu of any of the six photos.
- Can add and edit lifestyle characteristics such as gender, height, location, ethnicity, kids, family plans, politics, drinking, smoking, marijuana, and drugs.
- Can also include some basic information about yourself like work, job title, school, education level, religious beliefs, and hometown.
- Can link your Instagram account

THE LEAGUE

Designed specifically for those who are attending or have attended prestigious universities, the League offers the expectation to meet educated and successful people. The site verifies this when you grant access to both your Facebook and LinkedIn profiles. The site then creates a profile for you from your photos and information you provided on the sites. This is a more targeted site, which is useful to those with very high standards based strictly on academia.

- Wait list for approval of your application
- Pay a fee to avoid waiting
- Protects your privacy by blocking your Facebook friends and LinkedIn contacts
- A handful of matches each day
- If both parties agree, it's a match
- Must stay active on the site or be removed if no activity for two weeks

POTENTIAL PITFALLS

It's easy to wander into trouble because of the convenience of mobile dating; it's readily available anytime, anywhere. The accessibility leaves you much more susceptible to someone catching you since you're likely to access the site from your phone without the privacy your home offers. This can lead to a friend, stranger, boss, or coworker watching you slack off or possibly even catching a glimpse of what you're up to. Additionally, since cell phones today have built-in cameras and video cameras, this can be tempting to use because they're so easily accessible.

It's important to understand everything with your cell phone is **traceable** directly to your cell number. This information includes any text messages, emails, phone calls, and pictures. Once someone has your cell number, they can research and access your information, such as your full name, address, and employment.

Whoever get this info can use it against you. If you're willing to take the risk, prepare for anything you say or send in any conversation to be publicized with your personal cell phone number attached to it. Your safest bet is to expect someone who you don't want to see it to view anything you type or send from your phone. At some point or another, this will certainly happen, so be cautious.

There's no doubt about it, the dating scene today is through your phone. Luckily, you have the tools and strategies to succeed in all aspects of dating: in person, online, and mobile. However, we can't caution you enough to read what you type before replying.

One aspect that can be funny or humiliating is the auto correct function on your cell phone. This function is like spell check on Microsoft Word. The only difference is that auto correct changes the word on its own and sometimes doesn't ask for approval to change it. You want to pay attention because things can come across a little different from what you intended.

CHAPTER 15

STEALTH SITES—HOW TO FLY UNDER THE RADAR IN THE ONLINE DATING WORLD

"Fair: a place where there is cotton candy and pony rides"

—Kyle Max

Not all dates have to be set up using the conventional dating sites or apps. You can also pursue men or have men pursue you on social networking sites. This has become a very common approach and not as formal.

If a random guy approaches you on a social networking site, it can lead to an uneasy feeling. You didn't expect this friend request on this kind of site.

In contrast, a man is more comfortable with any attention a woman gives him, regardless of when and where. So, remember, you can also reach out to men directly. These sites are great for women to find the right type of man they're interested in as well, since the men are not in dating mode, which leads to a more honest connection.

FACEBOOK

Facebook has become one of the most popular sites online. Its main function is to connect friends online. However, with a huge database of members and a lot of money, it has forcefully branched into various other arenas.

I have reservations about using Facebook to meet or connect with strangers online; it reveals far too much information (full name, location, photos, friends list, etc.). While you can limit some of these with privacy settings, Facebook is notorious for changing its policies and settings with little to no notice to their users.

For these reasons, I recommend checking your settings regularly and having as much of your information hidden/private as possible. This includes you wall posts. You don't need drama on your wall or your business on the wall for that matter. Simply put, this is not the ideal site to fly under the radar on.

However, Facebook does provide a great platform to meet men without being on an actual dating site. Adding a stranger as a friend is not as effective as messaging one with a quick note. It doesn't come across as odd, and many view it as more normal.

Since Facebook's goal is to connect everyone, it's common for people to succeed in connecting with random strangers, past friends, and exes through the site friend recommendations. This can be good if you want to reconnect with someone. Facebook can also be a great resource for those trying to reconnect with past flames, previous crushes, and those you knew though never talked to or pursued.

With their huge user base, Facebook can plug and play almost any idea for a seamlessly quick implementation to see how the users take to it. These have included adding video to the site, business pages to like, messenger apps, and more. The most expected move is into dating. The implementation may take time to perfect, though this is something to keep an eye on.

Site Specific Tips:

- This is the most personal site because each person provides their full name.
- This site allows searches that will locate people by networks such as city, college, high school, workplace, etc.
- Profile pictures are viewable by all on the site.
- If you do not adjust your privacy settings, searching a person's name through Google can yield a link to your profile.
- Facebook keeps *all* your information, including messages, so be careful.

TWITTER

Twitter is a popular site that gets a message out (referred to as a tweet) in 140 characters or less. It's convenient to interact with other users, view their tweets, post photos, promote business interests, and state one's own personal opinions. Many celebrities enjoy using Twitter to control the messaging of an event or item of importance, rather than an inaccurate report in the media. You can use it to reach men for dating purposes.

You can like others tweets with a heart or send them a direct message. Research the chapters on what to say to stand out and use this to your advantage. If the person has a large following, it will be difficult to catch their attention due to the overwhelming number of likes and messages they receive. With everyone treating it as a social networking tool and not a dating avenue, you can turn this into a distinct advantage in separating yourself.

Site Specific Tips:

- The more people you follow, the more followers you're likely to have in return.
- Retweeting a tweet is a good approach to contact someone since they receive notification.
- Keep messaging direct as Twitter members are on the site for quick reads, not a novel.
- Post valuable content to gain exposure and more followers.
- The more followers you get the more people you can reach.
- Don't be obvious and only follow attractive men, they'll see through that.

INSTAGRAM

Instagram is another very popular social networking tool that people use to highlight pictures. People will post their travels, new purchases, or other things they find significant in the moment. You can "like" the photo or comment on it, and they'll get notification. This is another great avenue to test your wit and post something that may catch a man's attention by standing out.

Don't simply create a profile with the sole intention of pursuing men. Remember, give and take. You should post pictures that can display your exciting/interesting life. Unlike Facebook and Twitter, this site that doesn't force you to post personal information.

Site Specific Tips:

- Owned by Facebook
- Site is mostly pictures; some with captions
- Editing and filtering features
- Any pictures from travel pics to new purchases, a funny meme, or life moment.
- Can "like" a photo or comment like Facebook

OLD SCHOOL THROWBACKS

FACE THE JURY

Face the Jury was a site that allowed you to rate another person's profile from 1 to 10. It was very similar to the site Hot or Not. Each member typically posted one of their best photos for rating. The key was a catchy screen name, a good headline, and pictures to stand out. Because this site was accessible to all regardless of location, the attention you got from people viewing your profile created a viral amount of activity for your profile, and the views quickly added up. With that momentum, messages followed.

Despite the site being small by design (never having more than two employees and three servers), it quickly grew to be one of the top 800 most highly trafficked sites on the Internet with more than 6 million page views per day.

There was a top-10 list on the site, which ranked the most viewed profiles on the entire site. One of the case studies from our *Get Women to Want You* book, Marcus, had, in fact, climbed to number one on the entire site. He compared it to going viral; once you're at the top of the list, the views and activity jump quickly, and you simply enjoy the ride.

MYSPACE

Myspace was once the dominant social site to interact. In fact, it was larger than both Google and Facebook. Remember, Tom?

Many of the characteristics Myspace possessed were and still are valuable to meeting others online, while flying under the radar. Today's sites and apps center around linking your real name and Facebook accounts.

The attraction with what Myspace offered was creating your own persona. People could create their own name for others to see, have music play on their page, and customize their page. It gave you complete control. Most sites today require linking to your personal information to create advertising specifically for you.

Despite being ahead of its time, there are valuable lessons to be taken from Myspace. Go with the flow, not against it, embrace change and create your profile to be memorable, always thinking ahead.

CONTROLLING WHAT IS VISIBLE TO OTHERS

Keep up on your privacy settings. Many sites are continually changing what they have access to, what others have access to, and what you can control. The last thing you want is a message on your wall or profile from an ex who is either not over you, which is embarrassing, or someone stating something you don't want others to know about. Below is an example:

NEW	FROM	SUBJECT	DATE
☐		Request to Approve	Apr 14
☐		RE: Checking in	Apr 10
☐		RE: Checking in	Apr 8
☐		RE: Checking in	Apr 8
☐		RE: Checking in	Apr 5
	1 -10 Results	1 2 3 4 5 6 7 8 9 10 11 12	

IN CLOSING

All these sites are the most popular ones, according to our case studies, to maximize your success. Use this information as a cheat sheet in understanding what sites suit your needs best and how to navigate these sites effectively.

There are many dating sites to choose from. In fact, new sites show up daily. The universal concepts in this section will aid you in your success, both in the present and the future. Just adapt to the man you're interested in with all this the information, and success will follow.

CHAPTER 16:
HOW TO IDENTIFY AND CLASSIFY MEN ONLINE

"We all get what we tolerate."

—Tony Robbins

This chapter provides insight about what to look for to identify and classify the different types of men online as both people and perspective dating options. There are six classifications; however, some men may fit more than one of these classifications. For example, the good-time guy may also be the right moment guy, the one you're interested in at that moment or the boring guy who may have substance. Ultimately, you decide whether the timing or mood is right to be interested in any or all these types of men. The goal with the streamlined approach to identifying and classifying them is to make decisions of substance easier for you to sort through the many different men online.

THE GOOD-TIME GUY

This man is not looking for anything serious and has no interest in settling down. His pictures are typically not top-notch and make him appear younger than he really is. These pictures can include pictures with his friends, him holding a drink in his hand, or acting out. He tends to party, go out often, and lives nights he often can't remember with people he may not meet again.

EXAMPLES OF THE "GOOD-TIME GUY"

THE BORING GUY

This man doesn't stand out. His profile is very bland, style is plain, and personality matches both. He may be a nice guy or be very intelligent, although without anything to stand out, he rarely draws notice.

EXAMPLE OF "THE BORING GUY"

THE EXCITING GUY

This guy stands out. He reeks of adventure and spontaneous trips. His profile shows he's comfortable within himself to know what he likes and dislikes, is well-rounded with life experiences, and his pictures highlight an interesting life.

EXAMPLES OF "THE EXCITING GUY"

NEW SIGN UP

The new sign-up guy is one to keep a close eye on. This is one who isn't damaged from dating sites and apps or grown tired of them yet. Many men get on dating sites or apps and either the overwhelming possibilities sidetrack them to trying just to have fun, or they get discouraged based on their lack of success. If you identify a new member, this is the perfect time to chat with him. If they reach out first (which is likely if you use the guidelines in this book), you're in a great spot.

The new sign up will typically be respectful and optimistic about you and women online, in general. This is a good thing. You should seek this guy out, whether he's contacting you first or not.

"THE PRO" ONLINE DATING GUY

This man has been on many sites and for a while. He's what many would consider a "seasoned vet." The easiest way to identify this guy is through his words and actions. He may acknowledge he has been on different sites, offer you tips, and give his experiences. He's also likely to be very smooth with his responses and quick to have a photo to send. Trust that this isn't a photo he just took and has most likely sent before.

SUBSTANCE GUY

This man is a quality person. He's not interested in the perception or appearance someone can portray. He's interested in the reality and quality characteristics they possess. He's very direct with questions and asks about topics of importance to him. This could include career, family, goals, etc. It's doubtful for him to try to pick you up as many other men would by complimenting you, offering you gifts, or inviting you over to his house a short time after initially talking with you. His lifestyle matches his beliefs.

RIGHT MOMENT GUY

In the right moment, men and women can act out. They may agree to go out on a date, go back to someone's house, or do more, depending on their mood and getting caught up in the moment. In the moment, it feels right. Afterwards, it could be a mistake. As a woman online, you can do anything you want, at any time you want. The only caution you should take is your safety and how you'll feel the next day. Many men have no shame. You can have fun, but don't do something that could impact you more than just a night of regret. Be smart with your safety, personal information, work information, and family information. Getting caught up in the moment is one thing; exposing your entire life to a stranger is much more.

EXAMPLE OF A GOOD PROFILE FOR A MAN

Below you'll see a profile that's a solid profile for a man. His pictures are spot on, leading to more interest after the initial catching photos. The title "Giving this thing a shot!" is relatable and shows he's new to online dating, which is a positive and the profile description under the About Me section is very well done. He's likable, is neutral, and appears to be a solid prospect.

Live&LoveLife   1 IM   5 New Matches

Home Searches Matches Daily 5 Messages

<< Previous Photo   Next Photo >>

More of My Photos

In My Own Words:

My Job: Sales

My Ethnicity: Italian American

My Religion: Agnostic

My Education: Some College

Favorite Things: Sports & Traveling

Live&LoveLife

Giving This Thing A Shot!

Active within past 3 Days
28 - year old man
Houston, Texas, United States
Seeking women 18 - 40
Within 60 miles of Houston, Texas

Interested In: Dating, Relationship

Relationship Status: Single
Have Kids: No
Want Kids: No
Ethnicity: Italian
Sign: Aquarius
Body Type: Athletic
Height: 6'1"
Religion: Agnostic
Profession: Sales
Smarts: Some College
Do You Smoke: No
Do You Drink: Yes
Do You Drugs: No
Do You Have A Car: Yes

About Me:

I am new to the online dating world. I enjoy traveling, hanging out with friends and family, and working out. I decided to join this site after enough urging from close friends, as I tend to work a lot and don't get out as much as I would like! I think online dating could be a good fit, as I am over the bar scene. I'm easy going, positive, confident and try to make the most of any situation! I love the beach, warm weather, listening to the radio, and singing with the windows down! Iam not looking for anything as it never happens when you do, though am going in with an open mind and to live life to the fullest!

Do you Match?

See more like him

Add him to favorites

Forward him to a friend

Block from contact

Block from search

Report a concern ?

Click on a word to see more profiles with the same word. Click in a "+" to add that word to your profile.

MatchWords are a way of finding people with common interests. Add your own MatchWords to your profile and get in the excitement now!

Things You Are
Both Looking For

Comparing your profile side by side is a quick way to calculate chemistry.

Yes	Age	Yes
Yes	Height	Yes
No	Eyes	Yes
Yes	Body	Yes
Yes	Smoking	No
Yes	Drinking	Yes

3 Favorites

EXAMPLE OF A BAD PROFILE FOR A MAN

The profile below is exactly what you don't want. His main photo screams desperation; he's exploiting a little baby to get attention. He clearly doesn't have the ability or originality to get himself. He's overly boring with his approach and the title "God fearing guy looking for the perfect girl!!!" is overkill. There are no perfect girls, and his stating this shows his clearly flawed mindset. His About Me section provides too much information, referencing his daughter by name and red flags are throughout, including, being on and off online dating sites.

DanTheMan

God Fearing Guy Looking For The Perfect Girl !!!

Active within past 3 Days
33 - year old man
New York, New York, United States
Seeking women 18 - 40
Within 60 miles of New York City

Interested In: Dating, Sexual Encounters

Relationship Status: Divorced
Have Kids: Yes
Want Kids: No
Ethnicity: Irish
Sign: Aquarius
Body Type: Bodybuilder
Height: 6'1"
Religion: Agnostic
Profession: IT Verizon Wireless
Smarts: Bachelors Degree
Do You Smoke: No
Do You Drink: Yes
Do You Drugs: No
Do You Have A Car: Yes

<< Previous Photo   Next Photo >>

More of My Photos

In My Own Words:

My Job: IT Wizard

My Ethnicity: Irish

My Religion: Agnostic

My Education: Bachelors in Computer Science

Favorite Things: Basketball and Football

About Me:

My name is Dan, I am a God fearing guy who loves to have a good time! I have a daughter who means a lot to me and I try to see her as often as I can. I love you Elizabeth! I work hard and like to play harder. I have been on and off of these dating sites and am just trying to find someone who is a good down to earth person and doesn't do drama!!

Do you Match?

See more like him

Add him to favorites

Forward him to a friend

Block from contact

Block from search

Report a concern ?

Click on a word to see more profiles with the same word. Click in a "+" to add that word to your profile.

MatchWords are a way of finding people with common interests. Add your own MatchWords to your profile and get in the excitement now!

Things You Are Both Looking For

Comparing your profile side by side is a quick way to calculate chemistry.

Yes	Age	Yes
Yes	Height	Yes
No	Eyes	Yes
Yes	Body	Yes
Yes	Smoking	No
Yes	Drinking	Yes

10 Favorites

CHAPTER 17:

THE IMPORTANCE OF AVOIDING
THE "FRIEND" LABEL

"There is nothing more common than those regretting the things they should have done. You either act or you miss your chance."

—Francis P. Lawley

The "friend" label is much different for a man and a woman.

A man is more likely to act if an opportunity presents itself with a friend, based on a lack of discipline and when their sexual urges outweighing rationale thought. He likes what he sees, he acts. This is true regardless of his age and stature in life. Think of the powerful, wealthy men who put it all on the line for sex, Bill Clinton, President of the United States; Hugh Grant, A list actor picking up a prostitute, Tiger Woods, and the list goes on.

A woman, on the other hand, typically is more disciplined to not act on her urges. She also has more difficulty crossing the bridge from viewing a guy as a friend to someone to have sex with.

The most important thing for a woman to remember is how a guy looks at you is how he thinks about you. For example, if he looks at you as hot, he will associate any thoughts of you with your hot/attractive appearance. If he looks at you as boring, he will associate you as someone not high on his list of women to reach out to if he's looking for someone to hang out with.

For this reason, first impressions and any encounter after are equally important. Strive to look your best and not get too "comfortable" because this will quickly lead the friend down the road. Sure, it may be more comfortable to throw on sweats and a hoodie, but a man feels no attraction to sweats and a hoodie. If you're going to dress casually, wear yoga pants, shorts, and a more fitting shirt. Men see physical features before any connection has a chance to materialize.

One of the benefits of being on an app or dating site is that when you're talking to someone online, the facts are out in the open. You both are on a "dating" site, not a making "friends" site. With that already established, you must differentiate yourself from the "friend" category when or whether you meet in person.

Guys don't want to hang out with women as "just friends" unless they aren't attracted to the woman or value the friendship more than their hormones.

Note: Very seldom will a man choose a friendship over his sex. Most men simply don't know how to. Guys have penises, and penises don't decipher between friends and possibilities unless attraction is missing.

To avoid falling into this situation, you must be on your A game. This entails dressing nicely, having your hair done, being nicely groomed, and looking your best when he is or may be around. Don't chance it; if he may be around, be prepared. Overdressing is okay; men appreciate it. Not to mention, it's always better to be overdressed than underdressed. Think of attending a wedding in shorts and sandals rather than wearing a nice dress and Jimmy Choo sparkling heels. Overdressing is likely to garner good attention; being underdressed will attract bad attention and unwanted stares.

Your goal should be to keep his attention as much as it took to get his attention. Frankly, it's much harder to keep a man's attention than get it.

FRIENDSHIP TO DATING/RELATIONSHIP

Despite the "friend" label not being impossible to overcome for a woman, it is something you're better off not falling into if you're physically attracted.

However, when you make your feelings or interest in a man you're friends with known, you're risking awkwardness, rejection, and the friendship.

In the rare scenario, when both parties agree to stay friends but hang out on a physical level makes them "friends with benefits."

Friends with benefits can work. Though, rarely do these people begin as friends, hang out, have sex, and then go back to being friends. The reason for this is that at least one of the parties has feelings involved, and most of the time, there's jealousy. In the movie *No Strings Attached*, starring Natalie Portman and Ashton Kutcher, they had an understanding that their relationship was strictly sexual. Both parties agreed to the arrangement because both were busy and not looking for a relationship. As the movie ended, feelings developed as they spent increasingly more time with one another, and neither party liked seeing the other with other people, even though they weren't in a relationship. The moral of this story is to limit the time you spend with someone if you're looking to keep it strictly sexual. If you go out to a movie, eat together, or even hang around with the person doing nothing, you're entering relationship territory with the expectation to "make it official" soon thereafter.

Friends with benefits rarely end on a positive note. Eventually, one or both people develop feelings, and it ends poorly. However, the opportunity to be friends with benefits is greater when you're not friends to start.

Men and women have feelings and emotions. You should always strive to be honest but considerate. Be honest with yourself too; the friend label can hurt you if you allow it to.

SECTION V:

DESIGNING YOUR PROFILE

CHAPTER 18:

THE DO'S AND DON'TS OF CREATING AN ONLINE PROFILE

"The only true wisdom is in knowing you know nothing."

—Socrates

Now that you've learned about identifying the types of men, how to have "it," changing your appearance to look your best, and which sites and apps are best for you, this next part will detail how to implement what you have to offer to get men to want you online and on dating apps.

Your online profile is like a resume. Since men are taking in information rapidly and make instant decisions to discard a profile based on pictures and information provided, you must be on point with what to include and not include.

Do's

- Have more than one photo
  <u>Reasoning:</u> Many people may be suspicious if you have only one picture and may wonder if it's a fake; they may also wonder if you have something to hide.

- Create a witty, eye-catching headline that's in good taste.
  <u>Reasoning:</u> First, the headline stands out and shows you have class and education because you're not speaking in slang and don't have misspelled words. Remember, your headline conveys a message. A good sample heading is "Giving this thing a shot!" It tells men you're new and a little hesitant, which they can appreciate. It also shows you're new to online dating, and they may be also.

- Post pictures of yourself that show fun, excitement, and something for everybody.
  <u>Reasoning:</u> This will not only stand out but make them feel more comfortable reaching out to you since you're providing them good information with your likes through pictures. Examples include photos of you running a

5k, traveling, playing sports, painting, attending a sporting event, photography, with pets, parasailing, surfing, skydiving, etc.

- Post pictures of yourself alone.
  Reasoning: Having additional people in photos increases the odds that you'll have a mutual friend with men who are viewing your online profile. They may ask this friend about how you know them, which isn't the attention you want. If the mutual friend has a bad reputation, you'll be guilty by association, which can lead to awkwardness if friends or family catch wind of you being on a dating site. If you're a more private person, this is more reason to post pictures of yourself alone. Additionally, if your friend is more attractive, you look less attractive in comparison.

- Post tasteful pictures if you're showing off your body.
  Reasoning: It's not as tacky. A picture of you leaning over obviously trying to show off your breasts is much different from a tasteful photo at the beach. A good photo should leave the person viewing the photo looking for more.

- Be likeable and non-discriminatory with your opinions or statements. Essentially, be politically correct.
  Reasoning: As men are sorting through profiles, they narrow down profiles based on what they *dislike*, not what they like.

- Emphasize common interests as your main interests. Remember, the goal is to be universal.
  Reasoning: When you have very specific interests that only 10 percent of the people share with you, you're eliminating 90 percent of your possibilities. Instead, state the specifics that include items most people can relate to. Recommended interests include vacationing, comedy movies, the beach, local sports teams, exercising, volunteering, etc. Being very vague with a little spice (here's a chance to add a sense of humor) is a surefire way to differentiate yourself further.

  Example: "One of my favorite things to do is vacation! I enjoy escaping to the warm weather, and my dream would be to visit Hawaii. There's just something about the warm weather that puts you in a better mood. And to be honest, I am sick of the snow, cold weather, and people who can't drive in the snow."

- State one generic like you have that's popular.
  Reasoning: This will increase the percentages of men who can relate to you.

  Example: "I also am a big Kevin Hart fan. Though the movies are usually about nothing, it's a nice change of pace from the typical stresses of life to relax and get a good laugh!"

- State something that tugs at the heartstrings.

Reasoning: It shows you're a decent person, and that holds a lot of weight with men, especially in the online dating world. You can't be insincere, though, as she will see through it if she thinks you're not being honest or are doing so strictly for attention.

Example: "In my free time, I enjoy volunteering. There's no better feeling than helping those in need. It makes you feel grateful for all you have."

- State the somewhat regular activities you enjoy.
  Reasoning: It shows you're active and provides additional items they can relate to.

  Example: "When I'm not working, I like to stay active by going to the gym four times a week, play in a kickball league, camp, and catch a football game on campus!"

- Include pictures with any pets.
  Reasoning: It provides another way for a man to relate, like your profile, and stand out. Not to mention, if your pet is important to you, you don't want to attract someone who can't stand your pet(s) or may be allergic.

- Monitor your settings. Some dating sites allow far too much information, specifically social networking sites that allow others to write on your public profile. Edit the settings so you can see the comment before allowing or disallowing it on your wall; these requests go directly to your email.
  Reasoning: You never know what someone may post, and taking this precaution protects you. You don't want tons of comments on your profile page, nor do you want to be a person who's the favorite of a lot of people. The reason for this is you don't know what someone may post on your page. Imagine one of the guys you're interested in writes on your wall about how excited he is to hang out that night. By changing your settings on common social networking sites, you can limit what others post and what they can see.

  Example:

E mail Settings			
NEW	FROM	SUBJECT	DATE
☐		Request to Approve	Apr 14
☐		RE: Checking in	Apr 10
☐		RE: Checking in	Apr 8
☐		RE: Checking in	Apr 8
☐		RE: Checking in	Apr 5
	1 -10 Results	1 2 3 4 5 6 7 8 9 10 11 12	

THE KEY

- Make it appear that you live life to the fullest. Who wouldn't like that?
- You always have a great time.
- You're comfortable with yourself and don't need anyone else in your life to be happy.
- You're very likeable and have a lot to offer as a person.
- Show you're a "catch," leaving little doubt that other men would be interested in you. The goal of this is to create a buzz about how great you are without saying it.

Men will ultimately desire to hang out with you and will feel attracted to how you live life, how much fun you must have, and how they would have a better time being around you.

DO PICTURES

Pictures should be tasteful. Below are some examples. They may not seem overly creative, but they stand out. You want to provide a picture that will make it easier for a man to start a conversation with you. The items pointed out below are some of the highlights, he could easily comment on.

"YES" PICTURES

Lace design – unique

Belt makes waist
look thinner

Look toned

Look toned

High Heels

Headband

Tank Top

Striped Pants

P
I
N
K

Tennis Shoes
with Pumps

Fashionable shirt,
while still being conservative

Showing off toned
body in a tasteful way

Form fitting

Blazer

Work Folder

High Heels

If you look at each of the six illustrations above, you'll see they're all eye-catching but leave something to the imagination. For instance, the woman is wearing an attractive dress and holding cotton candy, which is not a common item to have in a picture and should be an easy conversation starter, the other woman is holding a puppy while wearing a Michigan shirt, both of which are topics a man can use to start a conversation,. The picture with a woman in a dress and wearing heels shows nicely with the lace arm pattern, belt around her waist, and heels compliment the outfit and her body. The picture with a woman appearing to be in workout or casual clothing, shows she can look attractive without having to dress up, while showing she's in shape in a very under the radar way. The picture with a woman with an off-the-shoulder belly shirt with tight jean is not showing much skin, but it's clear by the outfit that she's in very good shape, and the business professional photo shows she can be attractive dressed up, while also being serious.

Below is a natural setting illustration showing skin. Despite it being obvious she is wanting to show off her body, this type of picture is tasteful and would catch almost any man's eye when looking through profiles or pictures. In contrast, people perceive a photo with a woman bending over to show cleavage as slutty.

Photos play an important role in maximizing your results on any online dating site or dating app. Photos are one of if not the first thing a man will see.

DON'TS

- Nude photos
  Reasoning: These are not necessary to send to anyone. They're easy to use against you, and you receive no benefit taking or sharing them.

- Don't post a photo of yourself with someone who is better-looking than you.
  Reasoning: Obviously, if they're better looking than you, it's going to make you less attractive to the person viewing the photo.

- Don't have your name anywhere in your profile. This includes your screen name, user name, and email address.
  Reasoning: You don't want to have your personal information available for anyone and everyone to see. There are crazy people in the world.

  Example: NurseJen702, NurseJen702@gmail.com, Hello, dating world, my name is Jen.

- Don't ever mention exes. Period. This includes your profile write-up, any email correspondence, why you joined the site, or photos you cropped them out of, etc.
  Reasoning: There's nothing positive that will come from talking about an ex and why they're an ex. Focus on the future, and men will appreciate that.

- Don't ever post pictures with an ex or any males, no matter how good you think you looked in the picture.

    <u>Reasoning</u>: It's not worth your good picture. You most likely have other photos, so use common sense. If you don't, you know a question will arise about who the guy in the photo is. Why bother?

- Don't have a tacky headline.

    <u>Reasoning</u>: Few people have a quirky sense of humor, and your goal is to appeal to the majority, not the minority.

    <u>Examples</u>: "Looking for my Prince Charming." and "Are you my other half?"

- Don't post a photo of you and any baby or kids.

    <u>Reasoning</u>: This comes across as exploiting the kid and is creepy.

- Don't post close-up pictures of your face.

    <u>Reasoning</u>: It isn't necessary, and if you do, it may come across as if you're trying to hide what you're not showing. Additionally, a close-up of your face comes across as creepy and makes it easier to find imperfections and reasons to discard your profile.

- Don't ever take photos or post photos of yourself at work. This is a common mistake nowadays.

    <u>Reasoning</u>: Privacy. A photo can tell a lot about someone, and taking one while you're at your desk can show items in the background that many would overlook. See the example in the following chapter of the guy sitting at his desk.

- Don't ever acknowledge any shortcomings in your life or bad luck you've experienced.

    <u>Reasoning</u>: It will come across as negative and depressing. People want to hang out with those who are positive and contribute positively to their life.

DON'T PICTURES

Selfie with anything or anyone noticeable in the back drop

Reasoning: This is particularly awful because it displays the lack of attention to detail by having a little child in the background. If you post a picture like this, how confident can a guy be that you pay close enough attention to other important details that could affect him?

Clothes that are not flattering to your body

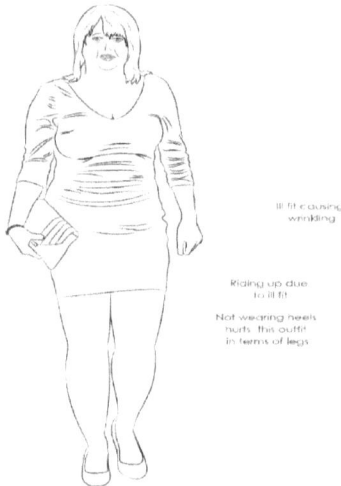

Reasoning: Not everyone looks good in everything. For this reason, you must understand your body type and positive features to show them. When you wear an outfit that shows your imperfections, the attention will focus solely on the imperfections, rather than anything attractive you have to offer.

Dressing slutty

No bra

Too short

Reasoning: Remember, not all attention is good attention. You'll likely be classified (fair or unfair) by how you present yourself. If you dress slutty, men will push their limits with you and have expectations from your outfit alone. Don't put yourself in that position. You can dress sexy without coming across as slutty.

Pictures partying or drinking period

Reasoning: This is your online resume for potential dates. Do you want people to view or treat you like a party girl? Party girls don't get the respect or treatment non-partiers do. Move on if you're serious about meeting men and getting men to want you.

Showing off your body intentionally (not in a natural setting)

Reasoning: It's fine to show off your body. If it's done in a tasteful natural photo, the majority will accept it. A photo like the one above is not tasteful and comes across as desperate.

A Different Perspective

Sometimes it's easier to understand how a man may view a woman. By using the same approach as you would when viewing a man. Look at the three pictures below. Note how underwhelming their clothes are, how sloppy the wrinkled shirt looks and how they don't catch your attention. You wouldn't be interested in them, so why would a man be interested in you if your approach is identical being underwhelming, not well kept, and standing out?

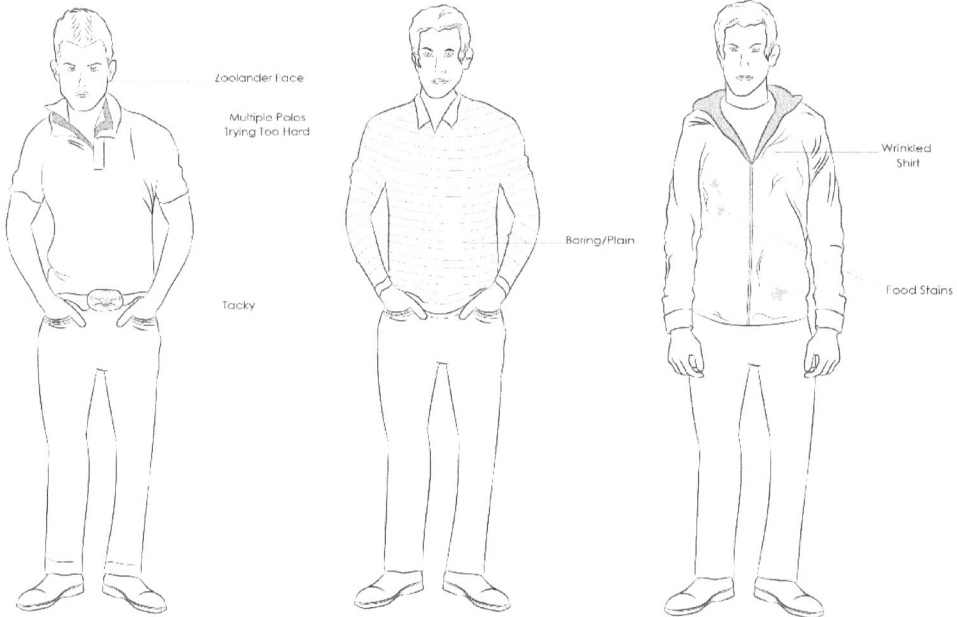

THE REALITY OF ONLINE PROFILES

- This is essentially your online job interview snapshot.
- Each person puts his or her best foot forward.
- Privacy is important for your safety.
- People will post old pictures.
- People will lie.

Remember you're marketing yourself to men, just as a company would market a product to consumers. While many companies market to specific clientele, your goal is to appeal to all men. You do this by avoiding any reasons for someone to eliminate you from the mix. Most men out there would discard you because of a bad photo or headline. Eliminate these bad pictures so they don't have the option to discard you by using the information provided in this chapter.

CHAPTER 19:
HOW TO DESIGN YOUR PROFILE FOR MAXIMUM RESULTS

"I am not trying to appeal to one particular girl. I want to appeal to all of them. I like more than one type, so why limit myself?"

—Website member

Your goal with being on an online dating site or app is to maximize your exposure through profile views and messages. You may not like or have an interest in most of the guys who contact you, but you still want to have them contact you to ensure you have a good selection. You may be looking for different things and different types of men at different points of your life. By achieving maximum results, you can then make the judgment call rather than alienating possible matches who have many other characteristics you might enjoy.

To maximize results with any online dating site and app, strive to be likeable. Avoid any controversial statements or religious or political beliefs because some will accept them, while others will reject them.

You should also make your profile stand out by having interesting pictures, a witty headline, and a condensed about me section. The about me section should display your fun, outgoing, adventurous personality, while being serious enough to show you have your act together, personally and professionally.

GOOD PROFILE

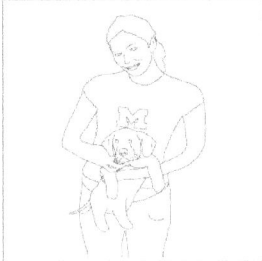

<< Previous Photo   Next Photo >>

More of My Photos

In My Own Words:

My Job: Numbers Gal!

My Ethnicity: Italian American

My Religion: Agnostic

My Education: Associates in Management

Favorite Things: My dog Stanley

NewYorkMacy

Why Not!?

Active within 24 hours
33 - year old woman
NYC, New York, United States
Seeking men 29 - 40
Within 100 miles of NYC, New York

Interested In: Dating, Relationship

Relationship Status: Single
Have Kids: No
Want Kids: Yes
Ethnicity: Italian
Sign: Aquarius
Body Type: Athletic
Height: 5'6"
Religion: Agnostic
Profession: Account Representative
Smarts: Associates Degree
Do You Smoke: No
Do You Drink: Yes
Do You Drugs: No
Do You Have A Car: Yes

About Me:

I think online dating can be a good avenue and hoping for success. I don't want to meet any more guys at the bar scene and I'm looking for a nice guy. I'm an easy going girl who makes the most of all situations. I'm confident, very positive and a boat load of fun!

I want to put it out there, if you're on this site just to meet new people, only make friends, just hang out casually and get some booty please DON'T contact me. That is not what I'm looking for. Although I am not opposed to becoming friends with someone after dating and getting to know them. And I only respond to profiles with pics Esp. those that show your personality.

My main struggle with this e - dating thing is I know I always get a lot more from meeting someone face to face. Emailing back and forth for what seems like forever and never meeting just seems like a waste of time. Either way I think you learn so much more about a person face to face.

Do you Match?

See more like her

Add her to favorites

Forward her to a friend

Block from contact

Block from search

Report a concern ?

Click on a word to see more profiles with the same word. Click in a "+" to add that word to your profile.

MatchWords are a way of finding people with common interests. Add your own MatchWords to your profile and get in the excitement now!

Things You Are
Both Looking For

Comparing your profile side by side is a quick way to calculate chemistry.

Yes	Age	Yes
Yes	Height	Yes
No	Eyes	Yes
Yes	Body	Yes
Yes	Smoking	No
Yes	Drinking	Yes

122 Favorites

BAD PROFILE

Home Searches Matches Daily 5 Messages

ArizonaAllie

Just Want To Have Fun!

Active within 24 hours
33 - year old woman
Phoenix, Arizona, United States
Seeking men 29 - 40
Within 500 miles of Phoenix, Arizona

Interested In: Dating, Relationship

Relationship Status: Separated
Have Kids: No
Want Kids: Yes
Ethnicity: Asian
Sign: Aquarius
Body Type: Athletic
Height: 5'3"
Religion: Agnostic
Profession: Management
Smarts: Masters Degree
Do You Smoke: No
Do You Drink: Yes
Do You Drugs: No
Do You Have A Car: Yes

About Me:

I am ready to be swept off my feet. I have been let down so many times, I question why I continue to let myself be hurt. If you are a cheater, keep on looking. I am always up for a challenge! I am a mommy's girl and love to party it up with my girls! I like to go out and enjoy a nice dinner every now and then. I am at the point in my life where I want to have as much fun as possible! I have been in relationships that have taken a lot of my time and am ready to get back to enjoying life!

More of My Photos

In My Own Words:

My Job: I'm very techy

My Ethnicity: Asian

My Religion: Agnostic

My Education: MBA

Favorite Things: Dallas Cowboys!

Do you Match?

See more like her

Add her to favorites

Forward her to a friend

Block from contact

Block from search

Report a concern ?

Click on a word to see more profiles with the same word. Click in a "+" to add that word to your profile.

MatchWords are a way of finding people with common interests. Add your own MatchWords to your profile and get in the excitement now!

Things You Are
Both Looking For

Comparing your profile side by side is a quick way to calculate chemistry.

Yes	Age	Yes
Yes	Height	Yes
Yes	Eyes	Yes
Yes	Body	Yes
Yes	Smoking	No
Yes	Drinking	Yes

412 Favorites

CHAPTER 20:
HOW TO ATTRACT YOUNGER MEN

"I tell you, if I'm going to go through a divorce, I would date a younger man. Because I have so much energy, there's no way an older man can keep up with me."

—Ivana Trump

The newest rage is for younger men to seek out older women, which led to the term "cougar." A cougar is an older woman who hangs out with younger men.

The reasons many women feel attracted to and seek out younger men is physical attraction, not dealing with the baggage that come with older men, the challenge, and feeling younger being with someone younger.

Immaturity, lack of common interests, and being at different phases in life can lead to difficulty interacting with a younger man if you're looking for anything more than fun. Some men may still be trying to find themselves and what they want in life. Simply put, their tastes and beliefs are unlikely to align with yours. If these are important to you, you must be a realist and understand this going into any interaction with a younger man. The odds are against having much in common. However, the physical attraction and the fun element may be enough.

Younger men need attention and training. Teaching them is telling them what you expect from them. Training may seem extreme but remember you're the experienced one. You can mold a younger man with little to no experience. This allows you to instill what's important to you, while not having to deal with bad habits many learn along the way.

For a woman to attract younger men, you must do the following:

- Don't talk about exes
- Don't talk about kids
- Don't talk about bad experiences
- Avoid relationship talk
- Be confident
- Talk as an adult, do not try to fit in with the newest lingo
- Mention having fun
- Be flirtatious
- Play hard to get

93

This book will provide you a universal approach to be attractive and get the attention of most men. By implementing the tips used to attract younger men specifically, you're good to go. However, many of the tips above are not only for your profile and about me section but also any conversations you have, both online and in person.

During conversations and messages, pay attention to the compliments he may give, questions he asks, answers he gives, and random comments. The compliments will provide insight to what he likes, for example, "That dress looked great on you." translates to he liked the form-fitting dress you had on, the color, and style. Any question he may ask provides insight about where his mind is, as do his answers. Most men don't overthink the meaning of what they say, they just get it out. So, by paying attention to what they're saying, you have a roadmap to what they like and dislike. Additionally, the random comments a man makes are insights into his personal opinions, whether he asks a question or not. Remember, you can't be the answer to someone's prayers, unless you know what they're praying for.

If you want to feel young again, this can be the breath of fresh air you so need.

CHAPTER 21:
How to Attract Older Men

"Up until age 40, most men are just not as mature as women. So, it makes sense that a lot of women date up in age a bit."

—Patti Stanger

If you're looking for more maturity, friendship, and companionship on a deeper level than physical alone, an older man may be a great choice. You'll find stability, experience, and a clearer vision of what they want in life. They have experienced enough to understand what's truly important to them.

The biggest drawbacks may be that they're set in their ways. This is more evident for men who have experienced financial success. Since they have succeeded, they're adamant their way is the right way, despite another way being better. They may also lack a sense of adventure or energy due to a demanding job.

Remember, older men are farther along in their career paths and can provide stability. Older men are typically more well-traveled, which can lead to traveling together and new experiences.

As with everything in life, there are advantages and disadvantages. The main factor with determining whether an older man fits your stage in life is to determine what you want.

Older men cannot put a price on feeling young. Their mid-life crisis involves spending money and taking drastic actions to feel young. One of our case studies, purchased a motorcycle and a sports car and got a haircut with fresh new dye job. None of this lasted because they were all temporary measures to feel good. Men don't like the feeling of getting old, and a younger woman is the perfect answer to their needs.

Men will spend money to impress a younger woman since he feels the need to, based on insecurities about his age. He will also go above and beyond to plan extravagant dates and trips.

For a woman to attract older men, you must do the following:

- Show off your youth through a carefree outlook on life
- Detail your adventurous side in your about me section

- Spin your youth and spin it as an asset in the about me section
- Have photos that show an active lifestyle
- Mention living life to the fullest
- Be flirtatious
- Don't be afraid to reach out to him first

If you're tired of immature younger guys and playing games, the older man could be a great fit for you. You should expect a deeper connection beyond the physical attraction and valuing different things in life. He's in a different phase in his life from yours, and his next phase will also be different.

CHAPTER 22:

THE SIGNIFICANCE OF TIMING

"Timing is everything."

—Old saying

Timing is everything. Timing can be the difference between someone taking an interest in you, giving you the time of day, ignoring you, laughing at your joke, deciding to hang out with you, or a multitude of other things. Timing in life can vary from wanting to focus on work, casually dating, not wanting a relationship, or wanting to commit and start a family.

Timing can break down into the late-night text, the late-night email, the late-night call, the late-night app message, and the rebound. Since we already covered the new sign-up, these four will have detailed insight about what the timing means.

The following examples are of how timing directly impacts late-night interactions with various modes of communication.

THE LATE-NIGHT TEXT

Reaching out to you at this level indicates his interest. If the person is texting you late at night and asking what you're up to, it's obvious he's bored and thinking about you. When someone is bored, they're typically looking for ways to occupy their time. Don't expect a man texting you being interested in anything more than fun, though. He's most likely reaching out to hang out that night, not ask you out on a date.

If you do interact and end up meeting that night, you should understand the expectations he has will be sexual. Understand his intentions and don't put yourself in a bad position.

THE LATE-NIGHT EMAIL

The late-night email is generally the same as the late-night text or phone call but without the urgency or clear intent to hang out immediately. However, with an email there's no certainty of a reply that night. Since many people have their phones with them all the time, when they receive a text or a phone call, they receive it as soon as they check their phones. Responses from an email could take a much longer time, sometimes the following day or even days later, depending on how often the person checks their email.

Text messages, phone calls, and app messages are by far the quickest ways to get an immediate response.

The most important things to take from a late-night email are that the man is thinking about you while he's alone at night. Also, he's taking his time to write you, so he's clearly interested. You can conclude that he's not doing anything or is already in for the evening if the time of the email is later than 11:30 p.m. Check the time the email was sent because that can provide valuable information.

There are three classifications of the late-night email regarding times sent and the rationale for each:

1. If he sends an email before 10:30 p.m., Don't look too far into it; it means he still has time to go out, meet friends, or go on a date.

2. If he sends an email between 10:30 and 11:30 p.m., he's most likely in for the night or had an early night after dinner. Most people are already out between 10:30 and 11:30 p.m., so chances are he did nothing or went out with friends, family, or even had an early date. He's reaching out to you at this hour because he wants to do something other than being on the computer at this hour. If he did go out with someone else earlier, his interest in them is not enough to stop him from reaching out to you. He's showing he's interested in hanging out with you.

3. If he sends the email at 11:30 p.m. or later, you can bet he has been out, maybe had a drink or two, and is either lonely or looking for fun. If he's reaching out to you at this hour, he's interested in hanging out. This could also lead to a fun night in together. The biggest issue with this email is it's an email. If he sent it in "real time messaging," i.e., a text message, a phone call, or an instant message, you could respond immediately to hang out that night. It's highly doubtful you'll be on your email at the exact same time, and if you were to respond immediately via email, it makes you look boring for being online or checking your phone at that hour. You never want to be the one emailing at this hour.

THE LATE-NIGHT CALL

The late-night call is not as common as a text, email, or message. It's much more personal and direct. When speaking to someone on the phone, there isn't as much time to write your response, and you must pay attention; it'll be clear if you aren't.

If you're receiving a late-night call, you can trust the person on the other end is clearly interested and not looking for games or delays to prevent seeing or talking to you.

THE LATE-NIGHT APP MESSAGE

An app messaging conversation can establish mutual interest, create excitement, and can be very effective to meeting men. A late-night conversation can escalate a meeting more quickly than a conversation during the day or early evening.

When you receive an app message from a man at night, it can lead to discussions about sex. Sex talks come about when someone talks about how long it may have been since they last had sex, how long it has been since they last dated someone, and why they're online rather than being out in the bar scene. Men are notorious for trying to direct the conversation on this path. If he's going this direction, you know he's simply looking for fun.

If this is the case, and you're 100 percent not interested, you should find a reason to end the messaging immediately. If he's more interested in fun than you, you simply are the option for him in the moment to achieve his goal. Don't waste your time.

THE THREE BEST THINGS ABOUT APP MESSAGING

1. You can have multiple conversations at a time, which means you can talk to multiple men at one time.

2. The second and one of the hidden gems about some, not all, messaging services is the ability to go "offline" while still actually being online. This is great for avoiding people you don't wish to talk to and for limiting distractions so you can focus solely on one conversation. The ability to message is still in place; the only difference is that others won't know you're online unless you message them.

3. The third and most important thing is that some app messengers allow you to organize the various men you're be talking to. You can do this by creating labels for each guy or creating groups. You must keep the different men you're talking to organized. For instance, an example of a name label would be "Brad 28 NYC Cop" If you follow that example, you can organize each man's name, age, location, and occupation. This is key because whenever you get a message from them, or whenever you message them, the title helps you remember who they are.

Unfortunately, many of their names on sites and apps do not provide any information on who they are to help you remember them. So, these labels are very important, and you should also use them when entering cell numbers in your phone, as well. One misstep can ruin an opportunity.

Examples:

Friends List

Josh 26 NYC Student – JMSamson444

Thomas 34 Dentist Upstate – TimmyMD

Alan 22 Tech Guy – NextBigThing2

Kevin 37 Sales Manager – CarGuy1976

THE REBOUND

You're on the rebound when a relationship ends and you're newly single. Most people tend to want what they don't or can't have. It's human nature. For instance, when someone is single they want to be in a relationship, or when someone is in a relationship, they think of the opportunities if they were single. As soon as someone starts to recover, they tend to act on past desires to make up for "lost time."

A man who is on the rebound looks at this as his opportunity to live it up. He was previously in an exclusive relationship and was envious of his single friends. Fresh in his mind are the crazy experiences his friends bragged about and the times he witnessed his friends go through girl after girl. Now, he can live the life he envied.

The rebound stage is like a person who married young and never got the chance to date or have fun when they were younger. They're looking for something new and exciting because most relationships lose the excitement and can become stale over time. It's safe to assume this was his experience as well.

Meeting or dating a person fresh from a relationship is a delicate situation. You must respect whatever happened before, not pry for more information, and direct any conversation. Nothing positive will come for the two of you by your talking about his bad experiences. He could still feel upset inside over how it all went down. What he needs to do now is to strictly have as much fun as possible. The issue with having as much fun as possible is this man can act irresponsible and borderline reckless.

Be cautious in dealing with this type of man.

If you're okay with this sort of setup (being a rebound date), then you can connect with him by not only being different **but better**. The most valuable thing you can offer him is a distraction. Plan an active lifestyle such as trips to the zoo, the mall, hiking, or a sporting event. It won't distract him for more than a few hours or the time you two are together, but this is very important for him to enjoy his time with you. As a result, he'll want to be around you more, and you won't just be a discarded rebound girl.

Avoid the bars. When a man is this fragile, one drink can lead to multiple drinks quickly. Some men can get emotional or irrational under the influence of alcohol. Stick to innocent fun things to do, with little downside or potential for issues.

SECTION VI:

COMMUNICATING EFFECTIVELY

CHAPTER 23:
THE DECISION-MAKING PROCESS EXPLAINED

"Think, decide, act; hopefully, in that order."

—Unknown comedian

As you understand more of how you and others think, you'll gain valuable insight into how decisions and thoughts are made. As you study these processes, relate them to your personal experiences. When you spot similarities, pay attention to ways you can adjust to learn better and improve your influence on others.

The following is an example of the decision-making process someone would go through in deciding to hang out with someone they met on an online dating site or dating app.

DECISION-MAKING PROCESS [9]

Situation Presented—Must make a decision in the given scenario.

Benefits vs. Drawbacks Evaluated—Weigh the benefits against the drawbacks.

Timing—The timing must be right. Include your location, current plans, and responsibilities.

Adrenaline/Excitement—As adrenaline/excitement builds, the benefit increases for the person to act in the moment.

Justification—Before deciding, the subconscious must build a case.

Availability/Ease—If the timing is right and it's convenient, proceed to the next phase.

No Roadblocks—Without anyone to intervene, the path to deciding is on the path to completion.

Commitment to Decision—The benefit amplifies, and the good feelings have taken over enhancing the commitment.

Action—Decision made, and any potential actions are complete.

Reflection—This is where potential regret for a poor decision or happiness from a good decision takes place. ext, let's look at the process of turning thoughts into action. The reason for the thoughts turned to action process is to gain insight about how humans decide when to act. This is a general outline for almost any action someone takes that may surprise you or seem out of character for them. The following provides insight into each stage.

THE PROCESS OF THOUGHTS TURNED TO ACTION [10]

Hesitation—At this stage they're not sure. They're too reserved and unsure to decide, doubt is present.

Frustration—Frustration builds because there are items they're not happy with.

Impatience—The lack of action to ease their frustrations amplifies the impatient feelings they have.

Desire—They have hope and expectations there's something better for them than the current situation.

Action—After enough frustration and impatience has built up, the light at the end of the tunnel appears in the form of desire and they act.

VALUABLE INSIGHT

Whenever you want to change someone's beliefs, you don't need to state your case but rather get them to question their own beliefs. Once someone questions anything, enough doubts will follow, and change is inevitable.

ONLINE DATING IMPLEMENTATION

So, you're thinking to yourself, "Wow, this is great stuff! Now how do I use this online?" The answer is, you type with intent. Since you have this knowledge at your disposal, keep it fresh in your mind. When you initiate contact (yes, women can reach out first, too; not all men have the courage to contact you first), understand their decision-making process. In doing so, you have a sneak peek into how to get what you want, a date, to hang out, and whatever you choose.

When a man does reach out to you first, you also will go through your own decision-making process, which has become so quick for you, you fail to realize how quickly you digest information. For instance, you're quick to discard a profile based on a profile picture, headline, about me section write up, or background information. Some women discard a profile within five seconds. However, if you're interested, let him know in a timely manner and add a smiley face at the end of the message to show you're interested. The man will hook quickly with a follow-up message to talk further or meet.

CHAPTER 24:
UNDERSTANDING WHAT TO SAY

*"Online gives you a distinct advantage on how to respond to a man.
You have time to think, read a message and make a decision,
whereas in person you may have to respond immediately, or it
creates awkwardness."*

—Anonymous

There will be times a man you're interested in is not reaching out to you. That's okay. You're one of thousands of profiles or pictures he has most likely seen or not yet seen online. For these reasons, don't feel discouraged. Despite someone telling you when you were growing up that you should never pursue a man, if you're interested in a man, pursue him. Send him a wink to begin. This should be enough for him to message you or email you. From there the ball is already rolling.

If you don't hear back from the wink, you should drop him a quick line such as one of the ones below:

- Hey, just saw your profile and you caught my eye! Let me know if you would like to chat!
- I am...(example of a common interest you have, that he has listed on his profile such as sports team, enjoyment of traveling, where he is from, etc.)
- I think we may get along, message me if you are interested ☺

It's important to understand the toughest thing for you to do is to get the conversation started due to the fear of rejection and overthinking various scenarios. The reality is you have everything to gain and nothing to lose.

Simply put, identify what you want and get it.

ONLINE

Most profiles will give you a cheat sheet for how to relate or connect with the man you're interested in. It depends on whether you're paying close enough attention to the details. This is clearer on the profile in terms of pictures, the headline, about me section, and stated likes and dislikes. However, some sites use messenger boxes (such as the one below). The box below illustrates information you can use to relate and connect with him.

For instance, this girl is clearly a soccer player or fan based on her screen name. The number 4 holds significance and could be something worth chatting about. She's wearing a scarf, so must be into fashion or somewhat fashionable and isn't interested in a much older guy, and clearly has little to no interest in younger men since she is 28 and is not listing any men under 27 as what she is seeking.

I know you're thinking, you just typed more about what she's looking for and described her more than what her profile states. You're right, you must do the same for men; deeper thinking leads to more insights. More insights lead to better conversations and interactions.

```
Instant Messenger Example

Soccergirl4: Hey!
Chadbro: Hey!
Soccergirl4: Whats up?
Chadbro: Not Much!
Soccergirl4: Hows it going?
Chadbro: Good!
Soccergirl4: Anything going on?
Chadbro: Nope, what about you?
Soccergirl4: Same stuff...
Chadbro: Ok, talk later?
Soccergirl4: Sounds great :)
Chadbro: Peace
Soccergirl4: Later

Soccergirl4:
```

```
Soccergirl4
28 year old woman
Los Angeles, California
Seeking men 27 - 33

Soccergirl4: Hey!
Chadbro: Hey!
Soccergirl4: Whats up?
Chadbro: Not Much!
Soccergirl4: Hows it going?
Chadbro: Good!
Soccergirl4: Anything going on?
Chadbro: Nope, what about you?
Soccergirl4: Same stuff...
Chadbro: Ok, talk later?
Soccergirl4: Sounds great :)
Chadbro: Peace
Soccergirl4: Later

Soccergirl4:

■ Save IM    ■ Block Contact    ■ Report a Concern
```

IN PERSON

Talking to a man in person can be much different from talking to him online. When you're typing on your keyboard or phone, you could be distracted or multi-tasking. He'd never know this unless you take time to respond. However, he'll know whether you're distracted, multi-tasking, or simply not paying attention. For these reasons, when you're face to face, you must pay closer attention to him. Make eye contact, don't look around, and keep your body language uncrossed; this includes your arms and legs.

The best way to communicate with a man is to understand how he best interprets information. Some men are visual (what they see), others are auditory (what they hear) and others are kinesthetic (what they feel). Determining how he interprets information is the key to connecting with him.

Armed with this information, you can see how which direction his eyes go to determine his communication strategy. For example, if you asked about his favorite memory, and he looked up on the right eye and looked down with his left eye, he is likely to be thinking back to a pleasant time and how he felt at the time. This could lead to a smirk or smile, as well.

By understanding how he thinks and communicates, you then can adjust how you speak to him in language he will easily understand.

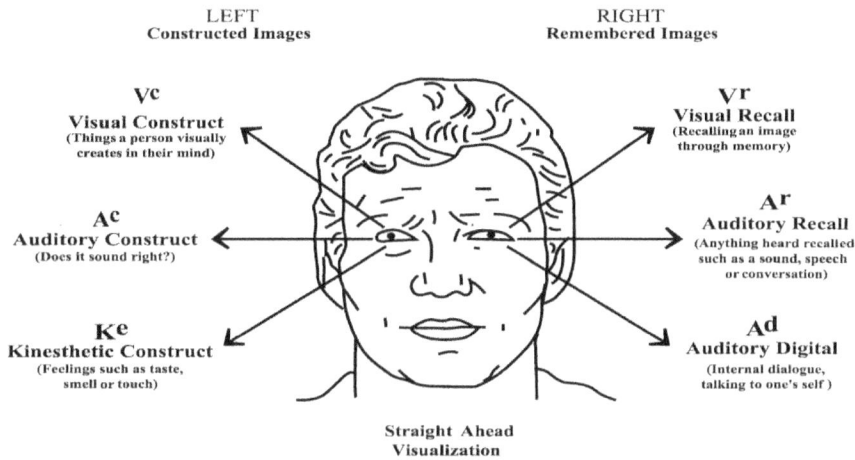

LEFT
Constructed Images

RIGHT
Remembered Images

Vc
Visual Construct
(Things a person visually creates in their mind)

Vr
Visual Recall
(Recalling an image through memory)

Ac
Auditory Construct
(Does it sound right?)

Ar
Auditory Recall
(Anything heard recalled such as a sound, speech or conversation)

Ke
Kinesthetic Construct
(Feelings such as taste, smell or touch)

Ad
Auditory Digital
(Internal dialogue, talking to one's self)

Straight Ahead
Visualization

Eye positions as looking at another person

CHAPTER 25:
COMMUNICATING TOWARD A GOAL
WITH COVERT INFLUENCE

"People are resistant to change. People are open to change when they don't realize they are changing."

—Unknown

Any conversation you have should have a purpose. That purpose may be to get to know someone better, occupy your time when bored, line up a date, or something else. If you're interested in hanging out or going on a date, then that narrative should lead your entire conversation to achieve your goal.

It's easy to get sidetracked, which leads to wasted time and not doing what you intended to do. Think of a time you wanted to talk to someone about something, only to leave the conversation not having said what you wanted to say. This is very common for topics you don't want to talk about, that is, the courage to ask someone out, the courage to end a relationship, or even firing someone at work.

In the dating world, your goals may range from getting him to ask for your number, asking you to hang out, come over to his place, or an official night on the town. If you don't have a goal, you're just talking. Talking with a purpose produces results. Results should be your goal.

Many men are stubborn. They have short attention spans and are shortsighted, but they do communicate their goal online. Most of the guys online have the goal of hanging out and having fun. In working toward this goal, they invest the time to chat, text, email, and even call.

You may be stubborn, too, but if you choose not to consciously stay aware of your goal while communicating, you're playing the lottery, and the odds are not on your side to get what you want.

Luckily for you, men are easy to influence. They cannot, however, feel they're being bossed around or influenced. For this reason, covert influence is a very powerful tool to have in your arsenal. Men don't like to be told what to do, so covert influence directs what they want but allows them to feel it was their plan all along.

The key to being influential is to influence without those you're persuading knowing they're being directed. Once someone feels they're being intentionally manipulated, they will react. Their guard will immediately go up, and they'll feel someone is pushing their beliefs on them. To implement covert influence effectively, you must identify how the man understands and interprets information.

You must implement certain words and language patterns in your vocabulary. You must also use them consciously on a regular basis, which will ingrain these words and language patterns into your vocabulary and daily communication.

We all have been in a discussion or argument when we knew we were clearly in the right and were beyond frustrated with the other party for not seeing our point. Some would think of this as arguing with an idiot. I call this everyday life.

While the right way or the right answer may have been obvious to *us,* the most effective way to get people to see our view is by changing how we communicate *our* message. It's important to understand you cannot and will not get someone to change their position or beliefs by telling them to change and forcing your beliefs on them. Presenting statistical data and examples are typically useless, too. However, getting someone to *question* their beliefs is the absolute most effective way to get them to change their beliefs.

Once they begin to question their beliefs, you create doubt, and a shift in their mind takes place. Often, this leads them to consider different viewpoints, and they become more open to outside perspectives.

So, you ask, how does this relate to online dating or dating apps? The answer is, if you two disagree strongly about something, getting them to question their beliefs often will lead them to seeing your perspective, which can lead to a change.

Another covert tactic is to ask questions that can lead them to the answer you want without giving away what you're doing. If they feel you're doing this, they won't like the feeling of being manipulated and directly insulting their intelligence. However, if you can get them to "see the light" on their own, they're much more likely to understand the other position and be open to changing their once-concrete stance.

Ben Franklin described his strategy for communicating his opinions while keeping rapport by saying, "I develop the habit of expressing myself in terms of modest diffidence, never using, when I advanced anything that may possibly be disputed, the words certainly, undoubtedly, or any other that give the air of positivity to an opinion, but rather say, I conceive or apprehend a thing to be so and so: It appears to me or I should not think it, so or so, for such and such reasons; or, I imagine it to be so; or is it so, if I am not mistaken. This habit I believe has been of great advantage to me when I have had occasion to inculcate my opinion and persuade men into measures that I have been, time to time, engaged to promoting."

I have hand-selected words that the book *Covert Persuasion* (by Kevin Hogan and James Speakman) lists as being crucial to implement into your vocabulary, while staying on course with your message:

You
Proven
Now
How
Easy
Fast
Imagine
Why

Free
Because [11]

You can use these examples above in the following ways:
- You know if *you* can make time or not to hang out tonight.
- It would be so *easy* to call in sick and go skiing today!
- *Imagine* the smell of the bonfire as we cook s'mores.

FIVE IMPACTFUL CLOSING OPENERS

1. I have to go, but you seem like a cool person...
2. I should go, though I'd like to continue this sometime...
3. I don't know how much fun we'd have as you....
4. You seem like...but
5. I'm more of a...

You can use these when closing/ending a conversation online and in person. By using these as closers, you're leaving the door open for them to disagree, which is what you want. If they disagree with what you're saying, they're playing into your strategy. For example, "I don't know how much fun we'd have as you seem more reserved, and I'm more adventurous and active." Immediately, the man will disagree and attempt to prove how he's adventurous and active, as well. They're trying to show how they'd be a good fit for you and you getting them to give in on what you like. Ultimately, this can lead to a more exciting time hanging out or date location since he'll want to prove himself to you.

LANGUAGE TECHNIQUES

Language techniques are the identification of techniques and patterns to be more effective in your communication. I incorporated some of my personal favorites with ones from the book *Covert Persuasion,* which are in the "Using Hypnotic Language Pattern" section. These language techniques are highly productive when implemented in the right manner at the right time.

I wouldn't tell you to...
How do you go about deciding...?
You might want to...
What is it that would help you know...?
You don't have to...
Imagine what would happen if...
Don't you feel...
What would it be like if you...?
Are you interested in...
If you were to come over...
Why is it that some people...? [12]

Another personal favorite is, I don't want to bother you if you have plans this afternoon, unless you really want to go to dinner at the new sushi restaurant with me tonight... The last part is very powerful since it's a direct command about *him really wanting to go to dinner at the new sushi restaurant tonight*. You can implement these however you see fit to get your point across. For instance, rather than stating, "You shouldn't go out to the movies tonight!" you can simply say, "I wouldn't tell you to hang out with me over going to a boring movie." By using effective communication techniques, you plant an influential seed in the sentence by inserting the direct command, *"hang out with me over going to a boring movie."* Direct commands are effective in getting your way as they speak directly to the subconscious mind.

PRESUPPOSITIONS

A presupposition is an implicit assumption, assuming something that isn't actually verbalized. The term *presupposition* is from the Foundation of Hypnotic Language Patterns.

Two examples of presupposition are:

1. "Once you put on your comfy clothes, you'll feel much more relaxed." This sentence is telling their subconscious mind how they should feel once they change, with the presupposition they change into comfy clothes. It's easy to see how this could help if you're trying to get a man to relax if he seems distracted, stressed, or upset due to any work or personal life reason.

2. "Hey, before we go out to eat, let's watch that new *Game of Thrones,* okay?" The direct message of watching the new *Game of Thrones,* followed by the "okay," acknowledges they'll watch the movie as well as go out to eat. The presupposition is they are going out to eat.

Often, the subconscious picks up presupposition without any second thought or questioning. A presupposition supposes beforehand. When you use this, you'll be amazed at the effectiveness of presuppositions and how often they're used in daily communication.

BOTTOM LINE

Using covert influence, persuasion, and language techniques can all be effective. However, you must be sincere. If you take a sincere interest in what he likes, your bond or connection will grow stronger. Furthermore, don't be afraid to step out of your comfort zone. Giving something a try and collecting new experiences, whether it be traveling, shows, music, food, or other activities will make you a better person who's more well-rounded moving forward. If this guy isn't the one, you'll be that much more impressive to the next man you meet. If it does work, by pushing your boundaries, the two of you grow together as a couple, which is a very special thing.

SECTION VII:

IMPLEMENTING YOUR KNOWLEDGE INTO REAL LIFE INTERACTION

CHAPTER 26:
HOW TO SEE THROUGH THE LIARS AND CHEATS

"Good luck is when opportunity meets preparation, while bad luck is when lack of preparation meets reality."

—Eliyahu Goldratt

Unfortunately, most people will lie on their online dating profiles. It could be fabricating their education, job title, or conveniently leaving out important details. They're also likely to post old pictures if they believe they look better in them. Other pictures posted may be misleading by the angle making them look thinner or more muscular than they really are, while others could be edited. Simply put, people want to gain an edge to come across as better than they really are.

RESEARCH BEFORE MEETING

The only way to identify these lies is by searching for their information online. You can play detective and see whether any information exists on their profile, profile pictures, screen name or whether you can get his cell phone number. You can type in his number on Google or Bing, and it can result with a link with his name and or company he works for. Additionally, if you have his name, you can search for pictures and job information.

As crazy as it sounds, you can and absolutely should search their names on the local court sites. Most counties have municipal court websites and clerk of court websites, which allow for searches based on their first and last names. As a result, you can view any court cases as minor as a traffic ticket or as major as a divorce or domestic case. Many of these sites will provide pertinent information, including their date of birth, height, weight, and address recorded. This is very important in case there are multiple men with the same name. This is not something you want to reveal to a man, but it's necessary. By doing this legwork you can prevent yourself from entering a bad situation or hanging out with a liar or a cheat.

Also, pay attention to his pictures. Men are notorious for not paying as close attention to the details as women. Below is a picture showing how easy some pictures men may post reveal information they may overlook, including their company's name, type of work, background which may be identifiable and a name tag or plate on their desk.

Judging Online Profiles

Men who post pictures with women are either ladies' men or wannabe ladies' men. This guy is most certainly a liar, talking to multiple women at a time or at least attempting to. Not all men who fit this mold are ladies' men, but that's only because they're not getting women to bite the bait. If they could, they would.

The profiles in which men refer to a perfect life and give a presentation that their life is great are ones to be very cautious of, as well. No one has a perfect life. Despite the friends you have on Facebook posting about how perfect their life is, they aren't going to post anything that wouldn't make them or their lives look great (to make others jealous, while bragging, of course). When men try to over-embellish their profile and lives, they're attempting to make up for shortcomings. This is the start of many lies, many disappointments, and arguments.

His pictures are also great to give insights into his current life. Pay close attention to the pictures on his profile and any he may send to you by direct message or text message, too. Below are some examples with commentary below.

If you receive this type of picture, be assured he has sent this to many other women, as well.

This picture screams insecurity. Despite being successful (they may not be his cars, or he may be in crazy debt), he feels this is the only way he can gain attention, not his personality, looks, or other features.

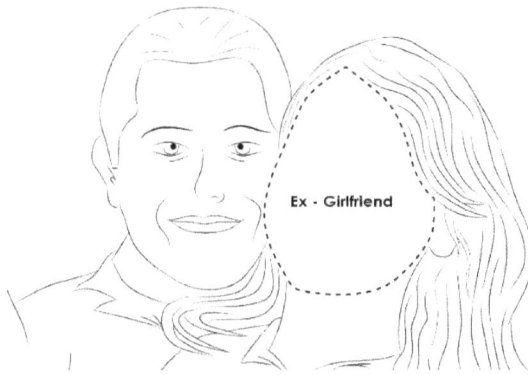

A man who posts a picture with a female on any photo, whether he blocks her face, is disappointing. Not only is it distracting, but it also shows he keeps pictures with exes (most likely an ex).

If a man posts a picture of himself drinking a beer or at a bar, he's clearly there enough to get a photo taken. Tread cautiously. Despite it not being as worrisome as a shot photo or bonging a beer, sitting at a bar is not an occasional activity for most.

This would make a great photo. If a man posts a picture that doesn't have incriminating items against him but rather shows him traveling and being adventurous, this is a true winner.

ONLINE/APP MESSENGERS AND TEXT MESSAGING

It's safe to say 75 percent of the time a man is online or on an app messenger (if the site states "online now") and takes a while to respond to a message, he's likely messaging other women.

Text messages get the benefit of the doubt; not all men have their phones with them at all times or check them regularly. Some are even model employees who put their phones away at work.

If they're interested in you, they'll be quick with responses. People make time for what they want to have time for. If they don't, they'll find an excuse.

If you two are supposed to hang out, and he cancels plans or always has an excuse why he can't keep the plans, be suspicious. Once or twice is understandable. More than that doesn't deserve the benefit of the doubt.

MEETING IN PERSON

When you do meet in person, pay close attention to where he suggests meeting or agrees to meet. If he doesn't want to meet at a location or a certain part of town, there must be a reason for it. Note it but don't make a big deal about it. Just remember it for down the road if the two of you talk further.

When you're talking, hesitant answers are a red flag. The reason for the hesitancy is his mind hasn't caught up to his physical reaction, and he's attempting to get his story (often lies) straight.

If you're out, and he's continually checking his phone, the easiest way to gauge the messages he's receiving is by observing his reaction to those messages. If he smirks or smiles and doesn't relay to you what he found to be funny or interesting, he's concealing it from you. The only reasons he would do it is a) it's about you, b) he doesn't want to engage you in conversation, or c) it's someone else he's infatuated with.

CONCLUSION

When you pay attention to the details, you have a distinct advantage over other women. Men are notorious for not being detail-oriented. They routinely forget to dot their i's and cross their t's, which provides opportunity for you to gain insights on who they are.

CHAPTER 27:
DECIDING WHERE TO MEET FIRST

"Over prepare, then go with the flow."

—Regina Brett

Your meeting location can create excitement, awkwardness, discomfort, enjoyment, pressure, and expectations.

- You may feel excited if you've wanted to check out a place but have never been before, or you're meeting at a place you really enjoy going to.
- You may feel awkward and uncomfortable if you meet somewhere you're not familiar with, a place you associate with bad past experiences, or do not enjoy the atmosphere.
- You may feel pressure and have expectations if you're meeting at his house.

Meeting at his place may mean he's automatically mapping out his moves. He does this because he's comfortable at his house, has most likely had women who've come over with the understanding that she's coming to have sex. While some women may be naïve, the reality is there's an unspoken understanding that if you're going to a man's house, both parties are willingly meeting based on intrigue or physical attraction.

Despite talking online, possibly by text and on the phone, this doesn't translate into knowing this man. He's still a stranger. You can stalk his profile, his Facebook page, and all the sites all you want, but just because someone hasn't been in trouble with the law (when searching the sites recommended in the previous chapter) or has glaringly obvious issues shouldn't put make you feel comfortable enough to meet him for the first time at a non-public place. You don't know this guy after all!

The temptation is great when talking to a man late at night to consider an invitation to his place or inviting him to your place. This is understandable. You may be lonely, interested, or attracted to him. The issue with inviting him to your place is he now knows where you live. Who is to say you may not like his looks in person and want to get rid of him? Better yet, what if you were just looking for sex and now this random guy knows where you live? These are not worth the risks, and both are very real scenarios.

For the sake of privacy, comfort, and safety, meet at a public, well-lit place. The place should have easy parking and have an atmosphere with a lot going on. Too intimate a setting with candles, dim lights, and quietness will be odd. A place that has live music, a good restaurant with a lively happy hour or a spot that has a lot of TVs with sports or music playing are all solid choices.

You want to be in a setting where there are a lot of people around in case he's a creep. A lively setting will lessen the pressure of small talk and creates a better atmosphere for enjoyment. If he's continually staring at the TVs or ignoring you, save face and cut the date short. Don't drag out the disrespect and apparent lack of interest. This should also apply to you. Some women are too nice, which is fine. They sit through a date with a man they have little to no interest in to not be rude. This is understandable and respectful. However, if you want to get out of a potentially bad date or situation, have a plan. You can do this by having a friend text you at an agreed upon time in case things turn bad.

There are also apps you can download and program to have a text message sent to you or a call, which can be a built-in excuse for you to have to leave immediately. Some of these apps are very clever. They allow you to program a name, pick the message you'll receive by text and the time to have it sent. Others are pre-programmed with the message or call coming from Mom or Dad among others. It's worth downloading for the just in case scenario.

CHAPTER 28:
UNDERSTANDING HOW TO CONTROL YOUR NERVOUSNESS

"Don't let the fear of what could happen make nothing happen."

—Doe Zantamata

Tony Robbins described NLP, Neuro Linguistic Programming, best in his first classic book, *Unlimited Power*. "NLP provides a systematic framework for directing your own brain. It teaches us how to direct not only our own states and behaviors, but also the states and behaviors of others. In short, it is the science of how to run your brain in an optimal way to produce the results you desire." [13]

The presupposition (there's that word again) is that we're all very similar, so if one person could achieve a result or feeling, it's possible and likely someone else can, as well. This doesn't account for intelligence, physical strength, or athleticism, but it does account for the likelihood of duplicating results through matching the steps someone else has taken through modeling.

Modeling is copying the exact same actions and reactions as someone to produce the same results they produced. These results can lead to great success, such as hitting a baseball or overcoming great sadness, when you copy the body language, reaction, and verbal response to bad news.

Think of playing baseball. The coach helps you hold the bat and shows you how to swing by lifting your front foot and stepping toward the pitcher while swinging evenly across your body and keeping your head down looking at the ball. To help you understand this, the coach will show you himself, so you can copy (model) his actions. If that doesn't resonate, he may get behind you and help you each step of the way. This is very effective and has been in use for years and years.

Now you may not care about baseball, but this is one of many examples of how modeling works from athletics to business to your personal life. The most successful people model others to perform better and improve areas where they're lacking.

Unfortunately, many also model the bad behaviors and actions of others. This can lead to rudeness, inconsiderate behavior, or criminal conduct. We all have seen generational changes, when kids get in with the wrong crowd or look up to someone who may not be the best influence on them and copy (model) their actions only to get in trouble.

When it comes to the dating world, it's perfectly normal to be nervous, anxious, and excited, all in one. You can channel the anxious and excited parts to not have a negative impact on you. However, some allow their nervousness to overwhelm them to the point of breaking down internally and externally.

To control your nervousness, you must identify what your triggers are. Triggers are situations or items that get you to the point of breaking down. You also must identify the steps you take to reach that state.

For instance, when a person gets nervous, they may begin to slouch with their shoulders rolling forward, head begins to drop, and eyes close, and they think back to a bad experience, which instantly takes them back to the bad feeling they had then. As a result, they feel bad and get more nervous or apprehensive about the future due to the uncertainty.

Each person can get themselves in a state differently. Clearly, not thinking or allowing negative thoughts or experiences enter your mind is a great start. To get into both positive and negative states, you take a specific set of actions, which you're most likely unaware of since it has become so natural to you.

The founders of NLP, Richard Bandler and John Grinder, believed there were three basic items that can be replicated to create the same results. They called them your belief system, mental syntax, and physiology. I differ in my titles and explanation somewhat, see below:

1. Belief System
2. Mind Influence
3. Body Influence

Your belief system

At the risk of sounding clichéd, when a person does or doesn't believe they can achieve or do something, they're largely right. A person's belief system can limit them most of all if they choose not to attempt something at all.

No one thought a human could walk on the moon, electricity could replace a candle for lighting, an airplane could fly around the world and a phone could eventually be with you at all times acting as your computer, camera, GPS, video camera, and more. However, once you do something once, others understand it's possible. Having the belief work to your advantage rather than disadvantage is important to your happiness and success in life. You limiting beliefs are more dangerous, so you must not limit yourself or what you can achieve in life.

To achieve anything, you must have a belief system that aligns with your goals. It's common to see those who have achieved great success look up to someone who was where they wanted to be. As a result, they altered their belief system based on what they proved was possible and decided to copy them.

Your mind influence

The mental syntax is how people organize their thoughts. Your mind influence is the information you feed to your mind and how you control thoughts. Your mind is just like your body, if you feed it bad food, you will feel bad. If you feed it good food, you will be healthier, feel healthier, and have more energy.

To have the greatest influence on your mind, you must implement what you notice to be most effective in keeping you on the right path, with the most limited number of distractions. Distractions and bad thoughts both take you away from the greatness you're destined to achieve. Perhaps the most powerful influencers in your mind are your friends and co-workers. People who tend to complain have pity-parties and feel bad for themselves. You cannot allow these people to be around you. Just being in their presence will impact you when you're not around them because your mind will drift back to the moments of their issues. Misery loves company. By refraining from being around these types of people, you're making a cautious decision to rid yourself of anything that will take up valuable, precious space in your mind.

Your body influence

Physiology is the way your mind and body sync with one another. If you're feeling bad, you can stay or get in that state by having your head see a sad face and thinking of other items that will make you feel worse. If you're feeling great, you're likely to have better posture with your shoulders held back, walk with a little more pep in your step, smile, and feel better internally as well.

The feeling inside shows on your outside, without permission. Some are better at not showing their feelings on the outside as much as others, though when you're upset or nervous your breathing patterns differ from when you're relaxed and happy. When you're upset or nervous, you tend to take shorter breaths and feel more pressure in your chest area. In contrast, when you feel relaxed and happy, breathing is the last thing on your mind. This is because you're in a great mental and physical state where both your breathing and pacing are not obvious.

You have a direct influence on your body with how you treat it. Eat right, exercise, don't abuse it with physical labor or mental strain. As a result, you'll notice the improved mental state resulting from a good-feeling physical state. If you allow negativity to influence your body, it will directly affect how you feel physically and weigh on your mental state, as well.

CONCLUSION

Simply put, the most successful people in the world have mirrored others to produce astounding results. Coaches are still helping the most elite athletes and executives to continually grow and learn. The learning and growing is necessary to improve. Most improvement comes through modeling. Be aware of your physical and mental responses and reactions. They determine how you feel. Being nervous is normal for most. Allowing it to overcome you to impact you negatively is not. The time has come to eliminate any thoughts and feelings that have limited you in the past or made you feel less than you desire.

CASE STUDY

One of our most successful case studies, Rachel overcame her nervousness, shyness and not knowing how to reply to messages by looking for things that were different with the man. If she was interested, she would comment about his profile, interests, and, most commonly, about his outfit or pictures. Below are various illustrations of men indicating things you can comment on to get his attention and start the conversation.

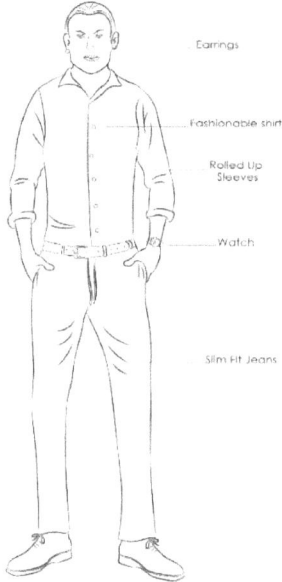

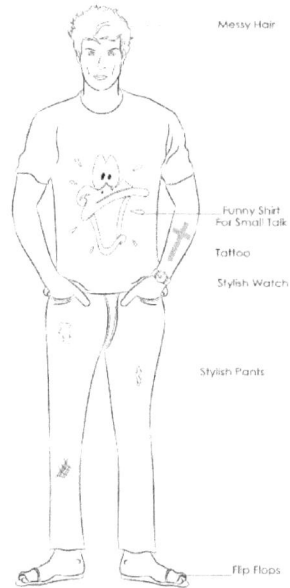

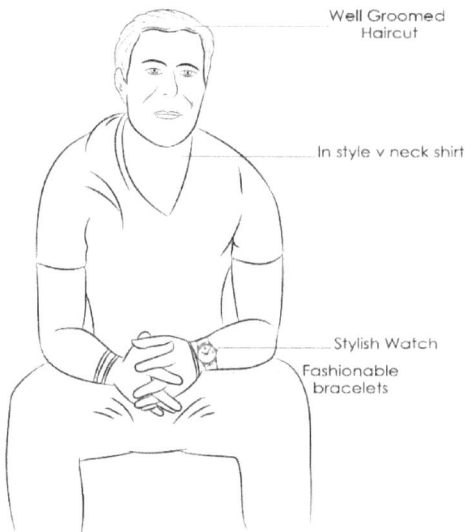

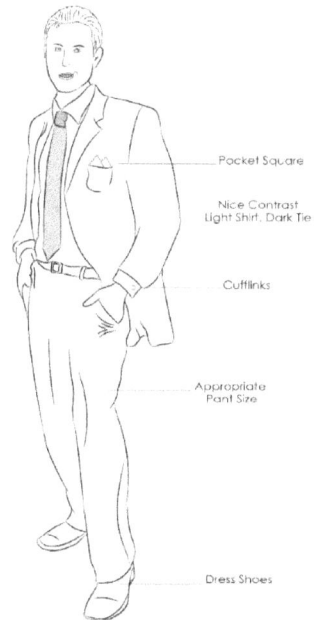

Earrings

Fashionable shirt

Rolled Up Sleeves

Watch

Slim Fit Jeans

Messy Hair

Funny Shirt For Small Talk

Tattoo

Stylish Watch

Stylish Pants

Flip Flops

Well Groomed Haircut

In style v neck shirt

Stylish Watch

Fashionable bracelets

Pocket Square

Nice Contrast Light Shirt, Dark Tie

Cufflinks

Appropriate Pant Size

Dress Shoes

Hat

Conversation
Starter

Fashionable
Vest

Rolled up
Sleeves

Nice Belt

In Fashion Pants

Dress Shoes

CHAPTER 29:
ALCOHOL

"A drunk man never tells a lie."

—Unknown

Drinking alcohol is one of the most widely accepted social activities. From an early age, kids watch their parents and others drink beer, wine, and mixed drinks. Some parents even allow their kids to have a sip. As their kids reach high school, they may drink alcohol in a social setting with their peers at a party. After high school, they get their first taste of bars, night life, and the college scene where happy hours, discounted drinks, and cheap shots are the lay of the land. Once they settle into their adult jobs, they drink after a long day at work or socially, as well. It's safe to say, drinking can find its place in any situation at any time.

The bar business is a great business to be in. When things are bad, people drink to get their mind off the bad, and when things are good, people drink to celebrate.

Alcohol means different things to different people. This is clear when you analyze how people casually talk about their drinking habits. The following are different phrases people regularly use, yet they all have different meanings:

"grabbing a drink"
"meeting for a nice glass of wine"
"looking to have a drink and relax"
"kick back and have a cold beer"
"getting hammered"
"want a nice buzz"
"needing to escape"

Alcohol helps many feel more comfortable, less stressed, and psychologically, it allows them to feel they belong. This is evident when you look around a room with alcohol present and see the socially awkward people always holding a drink in their hands. This doesn't make them less awkward, but it makes them feel comfortable when they're grasping that drink as if it were a life vest on the Titanic.

As a woman, you must view alcohol cautiously. The reason for this is because alcohol can impair your judgment and your well-being.

Men understand this, and they attempt to use your impaired judgment and well-being for their benefit. This is pathetic when you take a step back and think of the overall picture of a man feeding you drinks to get you drunk so he can get you to do something you're unlikely to do. Frankly, it's downright sickening.

Bars and clubs are notorious for offering drink specials, free admission, and nights dedicated to women. Their reasoning is that wherever the women go, the men follow. Since most men take the path of least resistance and have difficulty talking with women when sober, they use the drink specials or offering to buy her drinks as a way to garner good favor with her. This leads to more than one drink, offers throughout the night if she doesn't cut it off, and if it were up to him, she'd be drinking until she has difficulty standing. You've seen this time and time again, as have I.

Despite the urge to only blame the man for this behavior, the woman also assumes some responsibility since she didn't say no. She's the ultimate decisionmaker on whether she does or doesn't drink. She also must be aware of her surroundings as some men try to slip pills among other items in drinks to further impair her judgment. The best way for a woman to avoid being impaired or put in a bad position is to be responsible.

THE "FREE DRINK"

Men often give the free drink. They try to buy you a drink at a bar, a round for friends, or pass out "extra" drinks. Do not accept these.

There's no such thing as a "free drink." There are expectations with giving anything away. The initial expectation is your time and attention. Some men believe they're entitled to your number, a future date, or taking you home that night.

The bottom line is you don't need to limit yourself and your options by distracting yourself with a man who is essentially paying for your attention. Limit yourself to no more than one drink, if you have one at all, and pay for it yourself.

This way, you don't feel in debt to anyone, have to waste any of your time on someone you aren't interested in, or worry about what may or may not be in your drink.

CHAPTER 30:
HOW TO INTERPRET AND RESPOND TO MIXED SIGNALS

"Heart: Let's try it one more time. Brain: Let him go."

-Michael Anthony

Mixed signals can mean many different things. The reality is people want to have their cake and eat it too. They want to get all the benefits without any of the drawbacks of dating or hanging out with someone. This is most clear when there are mixed signals.

A man may say he wants to hang out, then flakes out by not calling you or holding to the agreed-upon plans. Another example is a guy may tell you he's not looking for anything exclusive, yet messages you regularly and wants to hang out with you often.

Mixed signals also exist when you're together in person. He may tell you he isn't like other guys, yet his trying to kiss you immediately and make a move prove otherwise.

Interpreting and responding to mixed signals lead us to over-think every detail. It's perfectly normal to over-think when attempting to identify and respond to a man; there's so much to consider. NLP master practitioner and trainer Steve Boyley, regarding reverse engineering, says, *"What has to be true for this to be true?"* The following are signals, moves, and reactions to assist you in understanding how to act.

- **Plans:** If you have plans and he flakes out, you don't allow this to happen more than once. The first time you can give him the benefit of the doubt, but you must convey to him that you cancelled other plans or rearranged your schedule, which you don't want to happen again. The reason for expressing this to him is to maintain your value to him and let him know you're not going to be there waiting for him.

- **Communication:** A man may text you throughout the day, send you an email, flowers, or even call. These are all actions of someone who's clearly interested in you. The constant communication is very similar to dating or being in a relationship. If you don't want this, you must create separation, which you can do by delaying your responses. If you respond quickly, he'll continue to reach out.

For a man to message you regularly, the expectation is he wants to hang out or go out with you. If his actions don't match his gestures, you can bet he's most likely messaging many other women, too. Don't allow him to waste your time. If he's interested, there's a chance he may not know how to close the deal by just asking you out. If you're interested, don't shy away from being the one who does the planning, and if he's interested, he'll quickly agree to almost any plans you suggest.

- **Exclusivity:** Most men would love nothing more than to date multiple women at a time, while each of those women don't date anyone else. Men can be jealous and possessive. They don't like the idea of having to share but love the idea of having as much fun with other women as possible. As a result, a man will talk a game that's one of commitment and interest to any woman he's with, but his actions contradict his willingness to commit or be exclusive because he has difficulty giving up the other women. It's not that he doesn't like you, it's just that he likes the idea of having you and hanging out with other women at the same time more. Don't stand for this unless you're comfortable with dating other men, too, and aren't interested in him enough to feel hurt or bothered seeing him with another woman.

- **Physical Actions:** When a man tells you how he's not like other guys and isn't a player, you take it at face value. The only reasons he would make such as a statement is if you were to mention not being interested in this type of man or if he brings it up as part of his differentiating himself from other men. Regardless, if he isn't like other guys, he'll be very reserved in his approach with anything physical beyond holding hands, hugging, or placing his arm around you.

  If he quickly moves in for a kiss or touches you on your body, such as your butt, leg, or chest, he's sending mixed signals, which indicate his actions are the truth, and the words are part of his game. Clearly, it's working since you're getting a man to want you, but this isn't the type of behavior you want to reward. Stop him and stop it before he thinks he can play you for a fool. You're too smart for this guy, especially after reading this book.

- **Smile:** A smile can indicate you're "nice," to express interest, or to blow someone off. A genuine smile is rather easy to identify because it's hard for a person to hide their facial expressions with a fake smile. It's important to view how he smiles and interacts with others to avoid total embarrassment. He could very well just be a flirt.

  If he's smiling at everyone else, too, proceed with caution. Also, identify the interest he gives you through his actions and mannerisms. Compare those actions and mannerisms with those he gives to others to gauge whether the attention you're getting is sincere or just his personality.

- **Body Language:** You can conclude a man is interested in you if he faces you without his crossing arms or legs. (The exception is if his toes point toward you while crossing his legs since he's still directing his body toward you). If he crosses his arms, looks at everything but you, is easily distracted, rarely makes eye contact with you in a conversation, or has his shoulders turned away from you, then you should cut your losses; these are all signs he isn't interested in you. If he's interested, he'll make it known 95 percent of the time through his body language. The same holds true if he isn't.

- **Hesitation:** If a man pulls back regarding anything physical, it means he's uncomfortable or has an issue with either you or the situation. Men rarely pull back or hesitate with women in physical encounters. They're known for getting nervous, but they don't just stop unless something is off. This something that's off could be lack of attraction to you, discomfort of the situation/setting, or his mind drifting elsewhere. The mind drifting elsewhere could be due to his mind thinking about another girl, a family problem, stresses at work, etc.

  Hesitation from a man can create an awkward encounter. If you experience this, ask him whether everything is okay. If he replies yes and you two continue, then all is well. If he replies yes, but everything stops, take this as a sign he's not a good fit for you. The only exception would be if he were to start talking about what's going on with him to give you insights about why he's hesitating.

- **Comments:** In any interaction, both parties are going to converse. Rather than just hearing what a man says, pay attention, and listen to his words and how he's saying them. His remarks will tell you how he thinks and what he wants. How he says it dictates his level of passion or interest in the subject. One of the easiest ways to understand the root of a comment is by asking yourself this general question:

"WHAT HAS TO BE TRUE FOR THIS TO BE TRUE?"

This open question can yield many in-depth and insightful answers that you can use. The key to asking yourself this question is to determine what he's not saying; there's always more to a comment or statement.

<u>Example</u>: "I'm not looking for anything serious."

What has to be true for this to be true?

He's obviously looking to have fun and not a relationship. He has most likely had women express interest in him for something more serious, and he avoids it for one reason or another. There are reasons behind his not wanting anything serious now. It could be his current career path, a recent bad relationship, his lack of time, his lack of desire, or the timing is not right. Identifying how he feels creates a clear picture for you, and you can decide whether there's an arrangement for both parties to be happy.

Example: "It was so boring hanging out with this girl I met last week."

What has to be true for this to be true?

He doesn't want to be bored. He's telling you he wasn't happy about the boredom. He's looking for excitement. This tells you that if you're boring, he won't hang out with you, either. He's telling you exactly what he wants, and that's excitement and something different.

Example: "I can't tell you the last time I could go out, relax, and have a good laugh."

What has to be true for this to be true?

He must not get out much. He has been busy so he's cherishing the opportunity to relax. His life is most likely too serious if he's grateful for a good laugh, especially if he can't recall the last time this happened. He's also acknowledging the fun he's having with you.

Mixed signals are a part of life. People shy away from making decisions and committing often. We see this with people trying to make decisions as minor as what to eat for lunch or deciding clothes to wear. We see the lack of commitment as attractive enough that large companies, including cell phone carriers and cable companies, offer no contracts. Since this is common, you must expect it and adapt. Those who adapt succeed.

CHAPTER 31:

TIME INVESTMENT—THE LONGER HE INVESTS, THE MORE INTERESTED HE IS

"Those who have invested the most are the last to surrender."

—Vince Lombardi

Time is the most valuable thing anyone has in life. You cannot buy more of it, regardless of your wealth. Each person has the same amount of time every day: 24 hours, 1,440 minutes, or 86,400 seconds. Since your time is so precious, you should guard it and be very selective whom you decide to spend any time with and what you choose to do.

As with anything in life, the more time you invest, the better you become and greater success you should have. In dating, it's a little different.

Time investment breaks down into three groupings for dating:

1. One time—fun
    a. Hook-up, have fun once, no future communication or hanging out, one date, move on
2. Repeat—hang out
    a. Casual, not committed, interested but not exclusive, fun is present, regularly get together, communicate semi-regularly
3. Future—interested
    a. Committed, interested, talk regularly, communicate regularly, exclusive

These three groupings are straightforward. The grouping we'll focus on is group three: future—interested.

If a man is truly interested in you, he's willing to commit or want to commit quickly. He recognizes you're a good woman, and he doesn't want to chance your getting away. When a man is looking toward the future with a woman, he speaks to her numerous times a day and wants to get together to do things regularly (not just having fun physically), and his mannerisms differ from a girl he may be casually hanging out with. He will hold hands with you, place his arm around you in public, kiss you in public, and not look around to see if anyone he knows is watching. This is because he doesn't care; he's into you.

A sure-fire way to find out if a man is really into you is if he introduces you to his family or wants to. Meeting his friends is cool, but that's not as big a deal. Meeting the family takes it to the next level.

The X factor with all this is the time investment. Some men will "put in the time" to get what they want. This is a part of dating and life. By keeping an eye out for the behavior mentioned above, you can determine whether he's just putting in time to get what he wants or whether he's looking toward the future, which he imagines with you in it.

SECTION VIII:

BIG PICTURE THINKING

CHAPTER 32:
IDENTIFY WHAT YOU WANT

"Success is getting what you want. Happiness is wanting what you get."

—Dale Carnegie

I was apprehensive at first when someone told me to write down exactly what I wanted in a partner. It's common to write down business goals or even write a business plan. It's surprising that not many have caught on that the likelihood of succeeding and accomplishing goals increases drastically by writing them down. Writing down goals and wants gives a person a picture of what they're striving toward. By writing down what you're looking for in a partner, you must decide exactly what it is you want.

This requires time and real soul searching. Many can easily say what they don't like, but pinpointing exactly what you do want requires much more effort.

You will attract what you write down what you want. Subconsciously, your brain will seek this type of man.

Below is a short five-point list to help you decide what you're looking for:

1. <u>Height</u>—insert ideal height range for a man
2. <u>Age</u>—insert desirable age range for a man
3. <u>Personality</u>—funny, serious, professional, reserved are examples to enter
4. <u>Hair Color</u>—bald, dark, light color, long are examples to enter
5. <u>Body Type</u>—thin, athletic, muscular, heavyset are examples to enter

This is a basic outline. You can always add specifics such as common interests (traveling, sports), religious affiliations, education, and career goals among others. Another important item for many can be timing. Women typically would like to have kids before 35 or no later than 40 at the max. This is understandable due to health concerns. However, you cannot allow yourself to be so focused on the age and not your goals. You can always change your expectations but don't allow yourself to settle on major items, including the type of person, a connection, and morals.

You should live your life to do better and be better than you were the day before. As a result, you'll get better and deserve better than you've received before.

In continually improving yourself, you'll do better in all aspects of your life. The outline for what you're looking for in a man is to give your mind a clear vision to focus on. Your subconscious mind will be seeking out men who fit your criteria. This sounds crazy, but I'm living proof to tell you it works.

When I was younger, I had a breakup, which I was pretty down about. I allowed myself to accept things I swore I would never put up with. Rather than having a pity party, I reflected on everything I was disappointed about for accepting. From there, I made a detailed list of what I was looking for.

As a result, I found the beautiful woman who became my wife. After dating for an extended period, I stumbled upon this list. Needless to say, it outlined her.

CHAPTER 33:
CREATING A BASELINE—
WHAT YOU'RE WILLING TO ACCEPT

"If you don't set a baseline standard for what you'll expect in your life, you'll find it's easy to slip into behaviors and attitudes or a quality of life that's far below what you deserve."

—Tony Robbins

Women put up with far more than they should. From rude men to aggressive strangers, women regularly deal with treatment they shouldn't. Unfortunately, since much of this behavior is so common, it's accepted as the norm. After reading this book, you'll have tools to cope with unacceptable conduct. Moving forward, you'll establish a baseline for what you're willing to accept in life. This includes dating, work, friendships, strangers, and from yourself.

The tips below should help you define what you're looking for and the minimum you expect. There are examples to help you determine what may or may not be important to you:

Dating
- Meeting locations—reputable, safe, well-lit, populated, easy parking, comfortable with location
- Manners—polite, considerate, not rude, chews with mouth closed, cursing, etc.
- Consideration—time for responses by text or call, being on time for the date, etc.
- Respect—not invading personal space, touching without consent, etc.
- Feeling good—someone who makes you feel good and happy in their presence

Work
- Type of job/career—long-term goals, realistic expectations, and impact it could have on your future if things progress
- Motivation—hard worker, big dreams

Friendships
- Two-way street—dependable, including physical help, emotional support, a shoulder to lean on when upset, and an ear to listen when you need to vent

Strangers
- Interaction—respectful, no touching, no inappropriate comments, no invading personal space

Yourself
- Career—making a difference, achieving performance goals, opportunity for growth and future, etc.
- Personally— reading daily to improve mental strength, going to the gym to improve health weekly, meeting a friend for dinner weekly, visiting family weekly, etc.

REASONING

By creating a baseline of what you're willing to accept, you're drawing the line in the sand regarding your treatment and expectations. By increasing your standards, you'll increase the quality of life. People make time for what they want to have time for. If a man can't make plans or prioritize time with you, he doesn't deserve the time with you.

The fact is if you don't have a baseline, you're likely to accept far more than you should, put up with things you never should, and settle for less than you deserve. Remember, your goal is to get men to want you, not use you or treat you less than you deserve.

CHAPTER 34:
SEX—THE KEY TO RESPECT

"There are some things money can't buy. Morals are one of them."

—Anonymous

Talking about sex makes many feel uncomfortable. Sex is a part of life and can enhance a relationship or connection. Sex is good.

There are different types of sex and meanings to different people. Some view sex as an incredibly intimate interaction, while others view it as a fun activity with no need for a connection, just attraction.

Humans are like animals. We feel attracted to others and tempted to act on our desires. What separates us from animals (most of the time), is that we have some type of self-control or judgment if it isn't right or appropriate. These judgments can often lapse when the urge or desire is great enough.

In the dating world, sex plays an important role in deciding the type of interaction and expectations both parties have. For example, if you have sex with a guy the first time you hang out, the expectation from him will be if you were to hang out again, sex is likely. Many men may not call or want to hang out again after this, too. Dating or thoughts of a relationship aren't on his radar.

However, if you withhold sex, it makes the physical attraction take a back seat to getting to know one another. By going this route, you can determine whether you two are compatible, and if so, it will likely form a stronger bond without the benefit of sex. This is necessary for a solid foundation going into a relationship. Some will argue that you must find out whether you're sexually compatible. That's a fair argument; however, for a woman who's interested in more than a friend with benefits or a random hookup, she must decide how she wants to be viewed: as the good time/hang out girl or substance/quality/future girl.

Men tend to gravitate toward low hanging fruit. They like what's easiest, which often backfires on them. What is easiest typically does not equate to quality.

Morals, in this case, are how and what someone feels is acceptable behavior. Men that have them are rare. Women that have them have power. Morals go a long way. By displaying you have morals, some men won't invest the time because they see they're not going to achieve their goal of anything sexual quickly with you and they're looking for the easiest options. This works to your benefit since this is an important step in sorting through the men who aren't right for you. This will also eliminate a good percentage of men.

While many men may get frustrated if they don't "get their way" if they were to hang out with you, this frustration will not have much of an impact on you. This is because they won't stick around long enough to impact you negatively. This is where men can show their true colors because they'll stop talking to a woman if they don't see their goal achieved quickly. For this reason, the men who do stick around are more likely to be truly interested; they're investing a lot of time to get to know you and bond with you. Additionally, the time commitment indicates interest from a man.

Don't get me wrong, some guys will stick around to get what they want. This is a very small percentage of men, and there's a special place in hell for these guys! However, you must remain strong in not giving in to any urges you may have. You want to build a foundation for a relationship, so you must have a strong connection, enjoy one another's company, and, most importantly, be different (better) than other girls he's met. By your holding out, he'll continue to see you if he truly likes you. This will elevate the connection and enhance the attraction further.

Ultimately, you decide what you're looking for and when. There may be a time where you're looking to have fun, and sex may be something you want or are looking for without any commitment. Other times, you may be looking for a connection first, to exclusively date someone, or take the turn into a committed relationship looking toward the future. If fun is what you're looking for or hanging out without commitment, you can do this. If you're looking for someone long-term, you must use discipline and foresight.

CHAPTER 35:
BOUNDARIES—SET AND DEFEND THEM

"A lack of boundaries invites a lack of respect."

—Michael Anthony

Unfortunately, many men think it's acceptable to make comments about, touch, and make unwanted advances toward women. You have a responsibility to not allow this more than once. You *must* address anything inappropriate and unwanted immediately. If you don't, you haven't discouraged this behavior. You can use the examples below for these "men" to get the message.

VULGAR COMMENT

Response—Loudly state, "Excuse me! What do you think you're doing saying such a thing to me? You should be ashamed of yourself. This is *not* acceptable." Do this very loudly to embarrass him and make a scene. He should get the message loud and clear. If this is in the work environment, you should also go to HR or tell him if it happens again, HR will be getting a visit. He must know you're not playing games.

*If you're not in public, find a way to leave the situation immediately. He's clearly testing his bounds, and if you're uncomfortable, leave.

TOUCHING

Response—Slap to the face! This should get your message across loud and clear. I would also follow suit with the embarrassment strategy by being very loud, scolding him, telling him this is *not* acceptable, and making him very uncomfortable. Again, if this is at work, you should immediately go to HR or tell him if it happens again, HR will be getting a visit.

*If you aren't in public, you should immediately go to the restroom and bring your cell phone, and text a friend your exact location and ask them to call you in three minutes. The friend should understand the call is one in which you must leave immediately. This is where the Plan B/Exit Strategy comes into play.

UNWANTED ADVANCES

Unwanted advances are typically after a vulgar comment, joke, or touching. For these reasons, you must nip each of these in the bud the first time and immediately. If you allow one comment or one innocent touching of the leg, you should expect more boundary pushing to follow.

PLAN B/EXIT STRATEGY

You should always have at least one person know when you're going to meet someone with the exact details—location, time, name, etc. From there, you should have a Plan B/Exit Strategy with one or two close friends with an identical story for when they may need you, or you may need them. The same story will make it easy to remember in a time of panic or cloudy thoughts, for example, a flat tire, house broken into, etc. This will also keep you calm so it doesn't lead to the man overreacting with you leaving immediately.

BOTTOM LINE

You have a responsibility and role in this. If you allow yourself to be a victim, you will ultimately become one. Address anything inappropriate or unwanted immediately, even if it's a boss or person of authority. If it is, in fact, a person in authority, go to HR immediately and confidentially so you're not in jeopardy. This protects you in case he uses his future discomfort for his lack of professionalism and respect toward you as an excuse to rid you.

The things we accept become the things we regret. Don't allow anyone to get away with anything. Once they do, another attempt is sure to follow. Fool me once shame on you. Fool me twice shame on me.

CHAPTER 36
BE TRUE TO YOURSELF AND YOUR MORALS

"The surest way to lose your self-worth is by trying to find it through the eyes of others."

—Becca Lee

It's unlikely anyone will know everything you do—good and bad. It's also unlikely for anyone to find everything out. However, you know what you do and how you act. If you aren't deserving of a good man, you won't get a good man. You should get a good man or have good men want you because you deserve it.

To deserve it you must respect the honor code, which means no intimacy with married men *ever,* regardless of his status of being on the rocks, temporarily separated, or lonely. The same is true for men in a relationship or cheating on someone you're in a relationship with. Who's to say the married man is really separated or going through a divorce or the man you're cheating with isn't a cheater, as well. Think about it, what type of man knowingly hangs out with a woman who he knows is in a relationship. Do you honestly think he wouldn't do it to you?

Hanging out is different from dating, and dating is different from relationships.
Absolutely have fun while you're single, uncommitted, and hanging out. This is the time to have fun, date, and determine the types of men you do and do not like.

Dating is more serious than hanging out.
While the understanding of exclusivity isn't that of a committed relationship, people see you together, and there's a chance of running into someone you know. Your interactions are more frequent than someone you're just hanging out with by texting daily, calls, etc.

Relationships take dating to another level.
Relationship means commitment; you're discussing your future and trying to talk multiple times a day, often not as a necessity but as a feeling of obligation and habit. All the steps following a relationship entail further commitment to one another such as pets, housing, cars, and possibly marriage and/or kids.

None of the phases above should be a surprise. We witness friends, co-workers, family members, and strangers go through this natural progression regularly. What is a surprise is that many are willing to settle for less than they want due to self-limiting beliefs, lack of confidence, and time restrictions.

Pressure from others and you is inevitable.

You must not give in to the pressure and influence of others when it comes to commitment. It's within reason to give the benefit of the doubt to a friend's suggestion to meet someone, hang out or give a guy a chance on a date. Anything more than that must be your decision. Dating is too time-intensive to waste your valuable time on someone who you don't see anything with or like. Relationships are far too mentally, physically, and emotionally involved to allow you to settle for anything less than happiness.

Pressure can come from friends, family members, co-workers, and, worst of all, you. It's perfectly normal to freak out when you're seeing everyone else meet someone and take those next steps in life while you're left behind.

Remember, you're choosing to be left behind. Your choice is to find the right person at the right time. This isn't a sprint; it's a marathon. You're looking to make the right decision once, when the time comes. Those that hurry the hanging out, dating, and relationships typically end in failure. For these reasons, you must listen to both your heart and brain. Think of it as a checks and balances system. Both must agree to make sense of it, otherwise, hit the brakes and determine why they aren't.

If your goal is to get a good guy, understand he's looking for certain characteristics in a woman. These characteristics include:

- Classy—can take her anywhere without question
- Morals—trust in her but still have fun with her
- Manners—good representative of himself in public
- Supportive—there for him, best friend
- Past—everyone has one, but that's where it belongs—in the past
- Motherly characteristics—motherly to him when needed; motherly to children
- Independent—not dependent on him for total happiness, happy on your own, proven independence shows maturity
- Trust—confide in her and rely on her for issues big and small
- Intellect—smart, impressive to talk to, easy to connect in conversation, well-rounded, polished
- Confidence—secure as a person and in the relationship

Guys consciously and subconsciously look toward the future when they're dating or in a relationship with someone they can see a future with. They begin to pay attention to habits you have, traits you possess, and how you would be down the road, should you both get married, have kids, etc. This is a tough line for a woman to walk because she can come across as boring and bland if she's catering too much to the mother aspects, but she still needs to display the excitement, attraction, and draw of the single life at the current stage.

He must meet your wants and needs, too.

Clearly, you have wants, needs, and expectations, too. The nice thing for you is that men are "trainable" as long as they don't know you're training them. An example of this is if you want a compliment. You ask him directly for the compliment. As a result, he'll compliment you. You then give him positive reinforcement by thanking him, smiling, and giving him a kiss. There's little doubt he'll compliment you moving forward as he associates complimenting you with making you happy and receiving a kiss.

This is as elementary as telling a dog to sit and giving it a treat. It sounds too easy but try it and be amazed. It may take a couple of times to get him to catch on, but he will; training takes time.

Future Discussion Approach

The single biggest mistake women can make when talking to a guy is bringing up the future too quickly. Men traditionally do not think that far ahead. By mentioning the future too soon into hanging out, dating, or in a relationship you jeopardize him running. It's not that he doesn't like you, it's that he's either not at that point to consider it or doesn't see you as the fit for it at this time. A better approach is to wait until he brings it up.

I know what you're thinking, he may never bring it up or I don't have time to wait for him. Your first choice should be to have him bring it up and then you can take it from there as he shows his mind is already thinking in that direction.

The more likely scenario is for you to find an opening to discuss it casually without any awkwardness. This opportunity would be best with a casual comment or question after seeing one of your or his friends out. The dialogue could go, "Do you think he's really into her?" "How long do you think they'll last?" or play devil's advocate with an intentional question to dig deeper and see if he says anything personally such as, "He doesn't strike me as a guy who's going to settle down." A general vague question will give him the opportunity to answer, and the odds are great he'll say more than a single word response. His response will then provide insights into how he thinks and, in all likelihood, lead him to give his outlook on his future wants.

Long-term Vision

Love is powerful. When you love someone, you care about them as a person and want them to be happy. You're willing to do things for them in a selfless manner. Love is real; infatuation is temporary.

The reality is infatuation yields excitement, magnifies attraction, and makes the time together more enjoyable. It can make you feel young again with butterflies in your stomach and have you thinking about them throughout the day.

After infatuation, the connection is either solidified by love or dissipates. Over time, love may remain or grow stronger than ever, but the excitement and attraction can fade. This is very common. Of course, it's more exciting and more physically hot at the beginning of a relationship since it's new to both of you. After years pass, people tend to become complacent. Gone are the days of dressing nicely for the other person, making nice gestures as you did during the courting stage and keeping up on their health to look their best for the other person. This is not acceptable.

Relationships require work and attention. You cannot allow yourself or your future partner think or act like this. If you do, it starts down a path that can doom the relationship beyond repair. Both of you must build on the growth that has taken place in terms of love, trust, and experiences. Constant changes will take place in a relationship; the goal is to grow together. Grow together mentally, physically, and emotionally. Each of the three are equally important, both of you should pay attention to making the other person feel their best, be their best, and do their best.

Keeping a good thing going

It's no secret, the excitement and anticipation with a man is greater in the beginning than it may be months or even years down the road.

The reason for this is anything that's new and different is appealing to humans since it's uncharted territory. More important, though, this is where the men and women both make their greatest efforts to be the best and present the best.

If you work as hard on yourself during your hanging out, dating, and relationship phases, your relationship will be as strong as ever. Unfortunately, most don't put in the type of work and effort once time passes. They become comfortable, tired, and complacent.

In the earlier stages, you dress in nice clothes, make sure you look your best, compliment one another, do nice things for one another, and keep a calendar full of things to do. As time passes, a certain spot on the couch replaces the gym membership, inattention replaces the compliment, doing nice things becomes an afterthought or chore, and you're too tired to prioritize things to do together. Simply put, everything that you did for one another and for yourself at the beginning to make everything so great becomes a thing of the past.

Remember you want to feel good. You felt good when you dressed up, looked your best, and were on the prowl looking for guys. You were doing this for strangers. If you're lucky enough to land a great guy, you should do everything in your power to keep him around and interested. This effort will get noticed, and he will likely do the same for you. You should expect to grow closer mentally, physically, and emotionally. The attraction is still there, as are the common interests, you just have to keep the growth. Despite the perception, a relationship doesn't have to be the end of all the fun, excitement, experiences, sex, and growth. Prioritize your partner and your relationship; it will be worth it.

To keep the excitement alive and show the commitment you have for one another, you must continually grow. In growing, you're continually improving, working to be better and do better, which makes everyone better off. Dating and relationships take work and commitment. They also are give and take. If you aren't doing your part to hold up to what you were advertising at the beginning, you should expect disappointment at the end.

Be true to yourself. Hold yourself to a higher standard and be better, do better, and get better.

With online dating, you literally have no excuses about why you can't meet someone, why you can't find a good guy, one who has their act together, has common interests, etc.

With the help of this book and the insights provided, you have a distinct advantage over other women in understanding how to position yourself ahead of them, sort through men, use universal techniques to achieve maximum success, and live a life you've always wanted. That life may lead to a house with a white picket fence and kids or may be jet setting for a weekend trip to Aspen or to the Bahamas. You decide your future.

I want to personally challenge you to join a site immediately and implement everything you now know. Applying the skills and strategies you learned in this book will generate immediate results.

As the founder of IHU, The Institute of Human Understanding, I commend you for making the commitment to change your life. Welcome to your new life. Remember this moment. It will be a life-changing experience, and your life-changing experience will soon become the envy of others. Anyone can say they want to improve their understanding and results, but you did. Now take this information and live the life you deserve.

Until next time,
Michael Anthony

ABOUT THE AUTHOR

Michael Anthony is the founder of The Institute of Human Understanding. The Institute of Human Understanding believes that human decision-making is predictable, once the person's classification is identified and understood. Mr. Anthony is nationally known for his research and understanding of human interaction and reaction. The Institute of Human Understanding has conducted more than 10 years of research for this book.

The research includes understanding the psychology behind the different personality types, how to effectively communicate verbally and non-verbally, and interpreting body language. It also includes how to create a presence (the "it" factor), establish rapport, and analyze the details of real-life case studies.

Additionally, Mr. Anthony has traveled extensively throughout the United States and abroad.

He has worked with people from more than 30 countries, including the United States, Canada, Sweden, India, Australia, Saudi Arabia, Egypt, Jordan, Germany, the Netherlands, Costa Rica, Italy, Spain, France, South Africa, Russia, England, Pakistan, Mexico, Israel, Syria, Malaysia, Lebanon, Turkey, North Korea, Slovakia, Finland, Thailand, Brazil, Japan, Puerto Rico, China, and Singapore.

He is a certified Neuro-Linguistic Programmer after having completed intense training in the field of Neuro-Linguistic Programming. Neuro-Linguistic Programming details from a linguists' and physicists' perspective on how people think and make decisions. Mr. Anthony is also a certified Master Practitioner of Neuro-Linguistic Programming after completing further training and certification on the Master Practitioner level for effectiveness and practice in the field.

Mr. Anthony's vast experience includes psychology, human interaction, language patterns, sales techniques, training efficiency, communication strategies and dating interaction. The author has tweaked this book continually over the years as new advances were made. The final product is the result of years of research, development, and most importantly, human understanding.

THE INSTITUTE
OF
HUMAN UNDERSTANDING

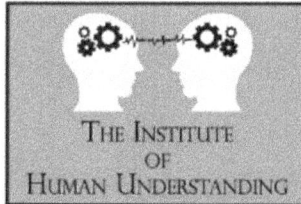

PRINCIPLES FOR SUCCESS

- Strive to be happy, not content.
- Do not ever settle; the things you accept can become the things you regret.
- Timing is everything.
- Don't acknowledge or participate in timetables for the sake of timing alone.
- Be aware of how you think so you avoid falling into past failures.
- The implementation of little tests (without the man knowing you're testing him) is essential.
- Knowledge without implementation is worse than implementation without knowledge.

WWW.THEINSTITUTEOFHUMANUNDERSTANDING.COM

REFERENCES

[1] *How to Marry a Multi-millionaire: The Ultimate Guide to High Net Worth Dating* p. 20
Ted Morgan and Serena Worth
Specialist Press International
New York, New York 2005

[2] *The Power of Charm: How to Win Anyone Over in Any Situation* pp. 38-62
Brian Tracy and Ron Arden
Amacom
New York, New York 2006

[3] *Silent Messages: Implicit Communication of Emotions and Attitudes*
Albert Mehrabian
Wadsworth
Belmont, CA: 1981

[4] *Kinesics and Context: Essays on Body Motion Communication*
Ray L. Birdwhistell
University of Pennsylvania Press
Philadelphia, PA 1970

[5] *Winning!: Using Lawyers' Courtroom Techniques to Get Your Way in Everyday Situations* p. 42
Noelle C. Nelson, PhD
Prentice-Hall
Paramus, New Jersey 1997

[6] *All the Rules: Time-tested Secrets for Capturing the Heart of Mr. Right* p.15
Ellen Fein and Sherrie Schneider
Warner Books
New York, New York 1995

[7] Site: www.Divorcestatistics.org
Link: http://www.Divorcestatistics.org

[8] Site: www.Marriage101.org
Link: http://www.Marriage101.org/Divorce-Rates-In-America/

[9] *The Institute of Human Understanding*
www.TheInstituteOfHumanUnderstanding.com

[10] The Institute of Human Understanding
www.TheInstituteOfHumanUnderstanding.com

[11] *Covert Persuasion: Psychological Tactics and Tricks to Win the Game* p. 211
Kevin Hogan and James Speakman
John Wiley & Sons
Hoboken, New Jersey 2006

[12] *Covert Persuasion: Psychological Tactics and Tricks to Win the Game* pp. 81, 213
Kevin Hogan and James Speakman
John Wiley & Sons
Hoboken, New Jersey 2006

[13] *Unlimited Power* p. 39
Tony Robbins
Simon and Schuster
New York, New York 1986

.

www.ingramcontent.com/pod-product-compliance
Lightning Source LLC
LaVergne TN
LVHW081323060426
835511LV00011B/1828